Trust 2nd Edition

Begins and ends with self

CONOR O'MALLEY

To Paula, Sean and Charlotte,
who helped me find my new cheese.

Edition two is dedicated to the surgeons,
anaesthetists, doctors, nurses, ambulance crew and
all the ancillary staff at The Alfred Hospital and
Sandringham Hospital in Melbourne.

You, individually and collectively, saved my life in
September 2022 with a triple heart bypass through
your expertise and care. I trusted you in every
facet of my Seven Assessments of Trust and you all
consistently delivered on your commitments to me,
as well as to yourselves. Thank you ♥

Having spent two weeks in the care of the health
system, the importance of Trust in this arena
to create a high-performing system cannot be
overstated. If you work in this area, or are a patient,
I hope this book brings you distinctions to consider,
and stories to learn from as you spend time in this
sector. Trust between both parties is critical to a
high-performing and caring health sector.

Book testimonials

"Conor has led by example. He trusted himself to deliver when his D-Day moment came. From knowing Conor as a supply chain executive to now having him as 'my caddy', our relationship has evolved ... for the better. This book is a great read, IF you are up for the learning challenge of facing significant hurdles and some deep self-reflection. I have no doubt the lessons I have learnt, and will continue to learn, will be the cornerstone to being a better leader. Simply put Conor ... thank you."

Dave Fenlon, Group CEO and MD, BWX

"As a leader who trusts her gut, this book is a powerful reminder to do so. It is more than that though, it provided me with new concepts that ignited me into taking action, both professionally and personally."

Alison Hernandez, Managing Director Asia Pacific, RandstadRisesmart

"This book is a leadership caddy for your pocket – learning and self-reflecting from one of the best."

Anna Reid, General Manager Kinrise, and a next generation leader

"To live and work richly is to trust in all areas of our lives; professional and personal. This takes daily commitment to be an ever-improving version of yourself. Conor O'Malley gives us great guidance with his New Ordering of Trust to lead more effectively, build better relationships and achieve your purpose."

Bill McTigue, Sports Physiotherapist/Director

"A structured model giving self-awareness as to *why* trust does begin and end with self. I found this book and its detailed model to be inspiring and it allowed me to ground my trust, consciously as well as emotionally. Conor says trust your gut; well the model allows you to trust your head, too!"

Joanne Drummond, Safety Consultant/Director

"I found *Trust – 'begins and ends with self'* a revelatory exploration of the whole concept of trust within a community, whether professional or personal. As an experienced leader of many years, I found myself reflecting on my own practice and preconceptions and, as a result of the focused and practical approach of the book, have become more aware of myself, my language, my actions and my 'Way of Being.'"

Simon O'Malley, Headteacher

Coaching testimonials

"Conor has materially changed the demeanour, communication, thinking and relationship management of some of Sportsbet's most senior people. Subsequent interaction has been more positive, cogent, and productive – leading to more profound outcomes than would have been achieved previously."

Barni Evans, CEO Sportsbet

"It is never an easy task choosing a coach for one of your senior executives. Striking the balance of some 'hard love' combined with an insight into how you want to release the potential of the individual are challenging. Conor found that balance, and I saw in the individual a lightbulb moment of understanding who they were and what they could contribute. There was a greater sense of confidence and a recognition that we were doing this because we saw this person's potential. It also built a greater degree of shared trust; trust in helping remove the person's anxiety and trust in the person's renewed self-belief in being at their best. It also left the person with ongoing support mechanisms that can be used on those days where, like all of us, they may not be at their best."

Paul Graham, Chief Supply Chain Officer, Woolworths Group

"Conor was instrumental in the development, and application, of an important Next Generation Programme for Family Business Australia & New Zealand (FBANZ), designed to inspire and educate current and future family business leaders. Conor worked closely with the FBANZ team, and Next Generational Members, to understand the needs and requirements of all parties before setting out the design framework and bringing in subject matter experts, including himself, to deliver what is truly a unique offering. The programme allowed FBANZ to value add to an important segment of the family business sector. Thank you very much, Conor."

Greg Griffith, CEO Family Business Australia & New Zealand

"Conor is absolutely brilliant at what he does. I don't quite know how he does it, but his ability to bring things out, give clarity, build confidence, and help you develop as a leader is second to none. He was always available and so genuine in his approach. I feel very privileged to have had the opportunity to work with Conor. Any of his clients are lucky to have him. Thank you so much!"

Anna Kavelj, Managing Director Woodhams Elite Relocations

"I can't recommend Conor enough, if you wish to grow as a person and as a leader."

Nyree Hibberd, Founder and CEO Koh Living

"Conor's program is well structured and delivered in a way that encourages you to challenge your inner thoughts and feelings. Conor's style is considered and sincere, creating an environment of trust as he takes you out of your comfort zone."

Ozan Kara, CEO, Netlogix

"The coaching and partnership I have developed with Conor has seen a fundamental shift in my thinking. Conor's approach is different. Having the amazing opportunity to build a trusting relationship with Conor has allowed me to reflect on my thinking and approach, while challenging me in a safe, trusting way. I have been able to turn these conversations quickly and easily into action, with amazing results."

Craig Lloyd, CEO, City of Whittlesea

"It was a privilege to have Conor partner with me and my Business Partnering and Planning team. Conor helped us re-set our strategic direction, and define our team values and behaviours, during the Trust Workshop that Conor facilitated, in the domain of Collective Trust. At a humanistic level the value that we co-created that day provided the opportunity for my team to reconnect. The workshop also enabled us to collectively, and individually, discuss, agree and define the value that we want to deliver to our business, including our intention, and the manner in which we would deliver that value. Conor, with his innate ability to build great relationships and put people at ease, was able to garner the trust of my team which was core to team engagement. Through this experience we collectively delivered a valuable outcome for both my team, and the broader business."

Robyn Longford, Head of Business Partnering & Planning, Officeworks

Acknowledgments

To Paula, my wife, for her unwavering support, love, and patience in over 30 years of marriage. Patience is, as you will read, such a core attribute to Trust.

To our children, Sean and Charlotte, for their love and trust in me. I am so proud of the young adults they have turned out to be, and how their lives are unfolding, after such a big move to Australia, from the UK, when they were 13 and 10, respectively.

To my Mum – Anne-Marie – and Dad – Peter – for giving me the love, support, and experiences that I have been privileged to have had in my life. Amazing parents.

To my brother, Simon, for his love, support, and counsel over the years. A true friend.

To my broader family and friends, who have been there for me and, I hope, me there for them, over the years.

To Kath Walters (and her team), my book coach – without her wisdom, support, and counsel this book would never have made it off a whiteboard, after an epiphany at 4 o'clock one morning.

To Alan Sieler, my mentor and teacher, who most generously wrote the foreword to this book and guided me in some of its finer points.

To Ant Youds who introduced me to Alan Sieler and Ontology.

To all my 'first readers' of this book, for their time and dedication in reading the manuscript, and to Matthew Webber, author of *Fit for Disruption*, for his support, before it went to the publisher. Their comments and insights were invaluable.

To Michael Hanrahan (and his team) at Publish Central, my publisher, for taking a manuscript and pencil images and turning it into a published book.

To all my learning buddies in my Ontology Diploma, especially the Victorian cohort of Sandra Falconer, Murray Vincent, Dayane Mardesich, Elise McSweeney along with Deanne Duncombe, as well as 'book club' member Marion Walker; my fellow learners on Julie Birtles' Leadership Programme and those teachers and fellow students on the 'Coaches Rising' Programmes who, in the last three and a half years have been an invaluable part of me 'finding my new cheese'. I include here those other coaches I have met and learned from outside of those specific learning domains, especially Gill Green, Deb Pascoe and Mairead Veeneklaas; also those associated with the Thought Leaders Business School in Melbourne – even though I have not been in that tribe, I have learned so much from their teachings about creating a Coaching Practice.

To my clients, whom without their investment in my service to them, I would not be where I am today and would not have been able to write this book.

To my colleagues in the Global Coaching Initiative who continue to work so diligently to bring the vision, in service of others, to life. I would also like to thank Magda Mook, CEO of ICF, for her counsel and support of me on this journey.

To the leaders I have previously worked for, the colleagues I have previously worked with, the customers and suppliers I have previously interacted with, and those I previously sought to lead, for their part in my life – both 'good' and 'bad'.

I make some other acknowledgments throughout the book, so as to put them in the context of a particular story or piece of learning.

To those of you whom I have never met in person, or who are no longer in my life, where my life, work and humanity has in some way been a part of your life. I hope that my being has created a positive impact and been of benefit to you. Where that is not the case, I acknowledge that, and I am sorry for any hurt or ill feeling that I may have caused.

Finally, I wrote this book on the land of the Boon Wurrung people and would like to acknowledge them and all Kulin nations people as the traditional custodians of the land that I live and work on. I acknowledge their special connection to Country and their care for the land, forests and waterways. I pay my respects to their Elders, past and present, and to all First Nations peoples and Elders across Australia.

First published in 2021 by Conor O'Malley.
Second edition published 2022 by Conor O'Malley.

© Conor O'Malley 2022

The moral rights of the author have been asserted

A catalogue entry for this book is available from the National Library of Australia.

ISBN: 978-1-922764-48-5

Printed in Australia by McPherson's Printing
Project management and text design by Publish Central
Cover design by Peter Reardon

The paper this book is printed on is certified as environmentally friendly.

Contents

Foreword

We all know just how crucial trust is in our everyday life. When we experience the absence of trust in family life, in the workplace, in social life and with our institutions, political and economic leaders, our quality of life is diminished. So much of what comprises the quality of our individual and collective existence is bound up in the quality of our relationships with others and the key institutions of our society. The absence of trust impoverishes our relationships and can significantly limit what we can accomplish together.

Trust is central to meeting the many challenges we face in all aspects of our lives, and in the bigger and related challenges that our societies face. Meeting these challenges is a collective effort by finding who to have relevant conversations with and being open to learn from these conversations. It is through trust that we grow and flourish through respectful, engaging and constructive conversations in which there is a desire to learn and not doggedly hold on to cherished perspectives for the sake of always wanting to be "right".

In the absence of sufficient trust our individual emotional, mental and physical wellbeing can suffer. In addition, our collective economic, social, cultural and political wellbeing can suffer. Habits of interacting that engender mistrust become consolidated and can form historical practices that become the norm, with blindness to the continued destructive consequences that play out. Individually and collectively, we become much less than what is possible.

Understanding and learning about trust has traditionally focused on trusting each other. While acknowledging that this is crucial, Conor O'Malley shares another vital perspective, which is the notion of trusting our individual selves. He does this from the novel perspective of Ontology.

The field of Ontological Coaching and Ontological Leadership is centred around the notion of Way of Being, which is where our perceptions and attitudes live and is regarded as the underlying driver of our behaviour and communication. In a nutshell, our Way of Being can be regarded as our inner self, aspects of which are not always easy to be aware of.

The most important relationship we have is with ourself, which occurs through our Way of Being. This relationship is the basis of everything we do, as well as what we do not do. It's the basis for being a parent, a leader, a coach, a spouse, a brother, a sister, and a friend.

Utilising his learning from the ontological approach to coaching and leadership, Conor shares how he learned to deepen trust in himself by making important changes in his Way of Being. Based on his extensive experience as a business executive, Conor shares how these changes in his Way of Being were indispensable to him becoming more trustworthy and effective as a leader. And his book does much more than this.

By outlining key aspects of Ontology as they apply to leadership and coaching, Conor also provides the reader with the opportunity to explore and make appropriate changes in their own Way of Being, as the means to develop greater self-trust and enhancing their trustworthiness. He shares the practical model of trust he has developed, and links this with related perspectives of self-awareness, interpersonal communication, and leadership.

Leaders can only get their work done through others, and this inevitably involves continually communicating, conversing, and relating with often a diverse range of others. Clear and constructive conversations and quality workplace relationships are at the heart of leadership effectiveness and organisational success. Conor's approach to trust is an important contribution to this much neglected aspect of leadership and how we are in relation to each other in all aspects of our lives.

Alan Sieler
Director, Newfield Institute and Ontological Coaching Institute
Author of *Coaching to the Human Soul: Ontological Coaching and Deep Change, Volumes I–IV*

Introduction

I have written this book for you if you are a CEO. In fact, for any leader who 'heads' an organisation that makes a difference in society – a difference both to those who buy or use the product or service on offer, and a difference to those who you lead. This could be a public company, private company, not for profit, a school, a law firm or accountancy practice, a consulting business – and on it goes.

I have written this book for you if you are a newly appointed C-level leader working in the same type of organisation as the leaders above and have recently been promoted to this position. You may be a technical leader who has been promoted to a more senior and broader leadership position, and you want to make an impact in that enterprise leadership role.

I have also written this book for you if you are a next-gen leader who aspires to lead an organisation.

Basically, I have written this book for you as a business leader making a difference to society.

Why should you read this book?

If you want to be an outstanding leader others choose to follow, as well as leaving a legacy while leading a fulfilling life, then understanding the role trust plays in all that will stand you in good stead.

In this book, you will learn how to trust yourself so you can trust others and build better relationships.

We all want to live in flow amid the fast-paced, complex and uncertain times that we exist and lead in. Trusting both your Way of Being and your Way of Doing will give you this flow in life. Things will feel easier.

I will share with you how to achieve this.

By learning and following my model, the New Ordering of Trust, you will lead self and communicate more effectively. This will support you, as a leader, to lead from the heart as well as the head. It will support you to lead others to get things done more productively, as they trust you more.

By learning and following my model and New Ordering of Trust, you will communicate more effectively. This will support you, as a leader, to get things done more productively.

Understanding the notion of 'collective trust' will give you more context for the importance of your changing leadership role in society, not only your organisation. It provides you with a framework to build trust collectively, as well as hold yourself and your team (or your business, if you are a CEO) to account, so others feel they want to trust you and follow you or do business with you.

Who am I?

I am a Scot, with an Irish name and an English accent, who is now an Aussie!

I'm a husband, father, son and brother who deeply cares for his family, and is now better at doing that because of what I share with you in this book.

I have changed my life, in part, because of what I will share with you in this book. I've changed it from being a leader in the supply chain with the intent of becoming a CEO, to becoming a trusted person who cares for others first, and who also happens to be a leading executive coach for CEOs – 'the CEO's caddy', where I walk alongside my clients on their learning journey.

I am a good friend to those in my life. And I hope that, as that friend, they trust me to be there and care for them and help them through the concerns in their life.

I am a golfer, a caddy for Ben Steven, a brilliant young player in my club's Pennant team, and a rugby fan of both the Melbourne Rebels and Scotland. Yes, in the rugby domain, I am long suffering! These are my two sporting passions. However, as you read this book, you will see that sport runs through my life.

As well as that, I am a learner – more open to possibilities and more curious now than I have ever been in my life. However, as those who know me well, know that I'm 'technically challenged' and at times a bit of an old fart (a very British expression for being old-fashioned in my thinking). My colleagues in both the coaching domain, and in the Global Coaching initiative, take me on their journey and show care for me, so I can absorb their new thinking and ways of working, especially with technology. As a learner, this is both a challenge and a pleasure for me. This book may just be that for you.

My D-Day

Let me tell you about my 'D-Day', the day in May 2018 that was the tipping point in my life between where I am now and where

I was at midway through this life-changing journey. I was in the early stages of my ontological coaching journey with Alan Sieler, who wrote the foreword to this book, as my tutor. In the company of my Victorian buddies and fellow learners on my diploma course, I was faced with a dilemma – hence, 'D-Day'.

I was slowly moving from a Way of Doing as a supply chain executive to a Way of Being that I was uncovering through my studies and changing life perspective. I was approached by an international search firm to see if I wanted to be considered in their search for an international CEO role in third-party logistics. This was my dream job, and what I had been working towards all my life. I simply did not know what to do given the choice I had made, or thought I had made at that point, with regards to leaving executive leadership.

I shared this dilemma with Alan and the others in our workshop one Saturday morning. Alan offered to work with me in a specialist coaching technique called 'dilemma coaching'. I asked the others if it was okay with them, and they all said, "Yeah, go for it. We want to observe and learn." Without going into too much detail about this technique and how I sat in three different chairs, openly sharing my thoughts on answers to questions, the outcome I had was an incredible moment of clarity – cognitively, emotionally, and physiologically.

Turning down this potential opportunity and continuing 100% with my coaching journey was the right thing to do. It was on that day – 12 May 2018 – that my irrevocable path to this book started.

As Alan Watts – known for popularising eastern philosophy in the western world between the 1940s and 1960s – is quoted as saying, "waking up to who you are requires letting go of who you imagine yourself to be". That is what I have done.

In terms of my professional credentials, I am a leading executive ontological coach who continuously studies and is accredited, through a graduate diploma, in the philosophy and biology of our 'Way of Being', through the Newfield Institute. I am a credentialed coach with the International Coaching Federation (ICF), as a Professional Certified Coach (PCC). I am also on the Leadership Team of the ICF here in Australasia.

I am the founder of CoachAid (more on that later). I am also an advisory board member in The Arts (Antipodes Theatre Company). I am a mentor for NAWO and work with the Board as a facilitator, where gender and diversity is valued and balanced in society. I also work with senior executives in career transition with RandstadRisesmart.

Previously, I was a supply chain executive, having had the privilege, in Australia, of being in the executive team of National Foods (now part of Bega), of leading both Coles' logistics and the 'local' operations of Glen Cameron's logistics business. Prior to that, in the UK, I was a Business Unit Director for Wincanton and the Operations Director for both Kleeneze and Matthew Clark Wholesale. I spent the first ten years of my career with two leading third-party logistics businesses, Christian Salvesen and Tibbett & Britten.

I now bring all that learning and experience to CEOs and leaders in their teams. This is done through a transformative coaching journey, to support those individuals to trust how they learn, lead, and know themselves more completely, so they become more effective leaders of self, of their team, of their business and in society.

My main message for you to consider as you read the book is:

"Trust begins and ends with self."

What's coming up?

- The chance to be the best leader you can be by knowing and feeling how trust begins and ends with self.

- Understanding why trust matters so much in your life, both professionally and personally.

- Introducing you to a new creation, which is both a model and a New Ordering of Trust that you can learn from, study, and use to bring more fulfilment to your life, both professionally and personally.

- Sharing with you a few stories that might make you smile, and perhaps grimace too.

- Giving you an opportunity to reflect on your life and what choices you have to take action on, to make some positive changes in your life and leadership journey, and not only relating to trust.

One

What is trust and why does it matter?

Trust is many things.

Trust has been ever-present as a basis of human evolution in society and continues to be so.

It is foundational to living a fulfilled life.

It starts inside your head, and it ends up in your heart.

If you ask me what my definition of trust is, it is this:

> *"That you consistently deliver on your commitments, both to self and others."*

Thereafter it is a twofold series of assessments, one related to your 'way of being', another related to your 'way of doing'.

I call the seven words underlined below the 'Seven Assessments of Trust':

> **Being:** *That you are <u>invested</u> in the concerns of the person that you want to trust, that you are <u>sincere</u> in this investment, and that you are both <u>vulnerable</u> and open yourself up to being <u>vulnerable</u> to the actions of that person.*

Doing: *That you are <u>reliable</u>, that you have the <u>competency</u> and <u>capacity</u> to deliver on your commitments.*

Both Being and Doing: *That you do all this <u>consistently</u>.*

However, it's so much more, as this book will share with you.

It begins and ends with self.

It is a choice.

It is a mitigator of risk in your life.

It's omnipresent. However, we often forget that.

Trust is fundamental to being a great leader and leaving a legacy.

Without going inside yourself and understanding yourself more, you won't find the true meaning of trust.

Consistently delivering on your commitments is how you will be seen, and trust is at the heart of how you are seen by others.

What's the evidence for this?

Imagine that you are regularly late in showing up to meet your friend for a coffee, and you're known as one of those people who's *always* late. Arguably, trust eventually will erode between you and your friend, if they place a higher order of respect (as opposed to time) with regards to you always turning up late. A more significant life example is delivering on your vow to someone else. With both of these commitments – meeting somebody for a coffee or making a vow – you're actually making them both to yourself as well as the other person. If you fail to deliver on these commitments, trust will be broken.

If you live in your head and not in your heart, then you won't find where trust comes from, and you won't be able to invest yourself in another human. Here's a question for you: How often have you thought something was okay and not felt, or you ignored, what was going on inside you?

As a leader, when have you felt most trusted by your team, by those deeper in the organisation, and even by your boss? I would argue it is when you've been more 'inside yourself' and understood yourself more. That is when you've felt most trusted and given most trust as a leader.

I'm going to give you my definition and some historical evidence of trust, including introducing you to the philosophy of Ontology, which underpins my New Ordering of Trust. Trust is ultimately when you consistently deliver on your commitments to self and others; and this comes from within, so we'll explore what that means too.

You need trust as a leader for others to choose to follow you. My definition of a leader is a person who others *choose* to follow, as opposed to *having* to follow. Typically, people will choose to follow you because, in part, you take care of their concerns, both personally and professionally, through your self-awareness, integrity and care for them. You may be their boss or their manager, however in my view you are a leader if people choose to follow you, regardless of your position.

With trust, your life is more fulfilled, and you'll leave a legacy.

Trust in human and societal evolution, and trust and ontology

Trust has been ever-present in human evolution and societal evolution. It's been a constant, and it's not something that we can take lightly or should ignore. We should be focused on it.

Trust has been a part of First Nations storytelling, through Greek mythology and Roman philosophy to contemporary 20th century writing.

The basis of my model of trust, which is a New Ordering of Trust, has its foundations in Ontological thinking. You need this context to understand where I'm coming from, and by sharing it with you in this chapter, we can move on without having to go too deeply into that as a philosophy again. We're establishing the ground rules here.

As humans, we need order. We need structure in our life. The way I've looked at my model of trust is an Ordering of it.

We trust stories in our culture, and we trust those who share them with us, who do this to teach us lessons in life. You will see the significance of this statement in the next chapter. As evidence of this take the Anangu, the traditional owners of Uluru, in the centre of Australia and their Tjukurpa story, that talks "about the beginning of time when ancestral beings first created the world" *(Parks Victoria)*. The Tjukurpa story, about the Mala people, has been entrusted to generations for its core message to learn from, which is, "that it is important to finish what you start and to watch and listen for signs of danger." *(Parks Victoria)*

Here is the story that is core to the culture of those who share it – the Mala people came from the North and could see Uluru and they declined to join the Wintalka people's ceremony (inma), who had come from the West, because their ceremony had already begun. Enraged at this, the Wintalka people created an evil spirit devil dog, called Kurpany, to destroy the Mala inma. "As Kurpany travelled towards the Mala people he changed into many forms. He was a mamu, a ghost. Luunpa, the kingfisher woman was the first to spot him. She warned the Mala people, but they didn't listen. Kurpany arrived and attacked and killed some of the men. In great fear and confusion, the remaining Mala people fled down into South Australia with Kurpany chasing them. The story continues down south." *(Parks Australia)* Story has it that "these ancestors are still here today. Luunpa still keeps watch, but she is now a large rock. Kurpany's footprints are imprinted into the rock heading towards the east and south. The men who were killed are still in their cave." *(Parks Australia)* This is a story that the First Nations people have allowed to be shared with visitors, by *Parks Australia.*

Our stories, and how they have been entrusted to generations to share, are at the core of every civilisation's beliefs – as can be seen above – and are at the heart of trusting self and others. You will see this throughout the book.

We know that trust is also at the core of Western civilisation. The Greeks had Pistis, the goddess of trust, and the Romans had Fides, her equivalent. Both these new societies of their day had Gods who were characterised by trust or figures of trust, which suggests that trust was important in the beliefs and stories of those evolving societies and civilisations.

The dictionary.com definition of the verb 'trust' originated circa 1200 with the Norse word *treysta*, which means to 'rely on, make strong or safe'. Trust is also a noun. The noun definition of the word emanates from the Norse *traust*, which is 'the reliance on the veracity, integrity or other virtues of something'. From an etymological perspective, that's the basis of the word trust.

The word and images of trust have been around a long time. They have been, and still are, so important to our way of life globally in society, and also to our 'Way of Being' personally. I will explore and explain 'Way of Being' later in the book.

I mentioned in the beginning of this chapter I would introduce you to Ontology, well here it is: "Ontology, the philosophical study of being in general, or of what applies neutrally to every-thing that is real." *(britannica.com)* Put more simply, it's a way to understand what is going on inside you and helps you see the world from 'an inside out' perspective based on: the language that you use, the mood that you are 'in' and the emotions that you feel, and the sensations that you notice in your body. The Ontological combination of these three – language, moods, and physiology – is your 'Way of Being'.

By seeing the world from an 'inside out' perspective by focusing on these three elements of your Way of Being, you will be more curious and cope with not knowing. You will create the ability to find your passion and enthusiasm in the moment as well as be more patient and have more perseverance – essential in my view to being resilient. You will find peace and acceptance with situations more readily, enabling you to take action in life that serves you, and those around you, better.

By observing your 'Way of Being' you will find the courage to be vulnerable and envision possibilities, which is vital to being an effective leader today.

The 20th century basis of Ontological thinking was Martin Heidegger's book *Being and Time*, written in 1927. This form of thinking was continued by Fernando Flores in the 1980s, who published a book *Understanding Computers and Cognition*, written in 1986, about how people get things done. His work built on other luminaries in different fields. In the field of existential philosophy Flores built on Martin Heidegger's work. In the field of biology of cognition, he built on Humberto Maturana and Francisco Varela's work. In the philosophy of language, he built on the work of John Austin and John Searle.

This area is now known as 'Ontology of the Human Observer', a phrase coined by world leading Ontological Coach and Facilitator, and Director of the Newfield Institute, Alan Sieler, in 1999, who I've worked with and as you now know, wrote the foreword to this book.

Later in the book I will share my distinction of 'way of being' along with my distinction of 'way of doing', and how combined they will enable you to be a more effective leader of self, of your team, of your business and in society.

Trust is a key ontological distinction referred to in the writing of Sieler. He writes that, "There are four elements of trust: sincerity, reliability, competence and involvement." **Sincerity** means I am truthful in my part of the relationship; **reliability** means if I make a commitment or promise then I deliver on it. When I make an offer, I self-assess that I have the **competency** to deliver on it, and **involvement** means that I am taking care of your 'concerns' (ontologically, 'concerns' are 'what really matters to you', not solely your worries). These elements come from his book *Coaching to the Human Soul, Volume One*.

You have to have the 'capacity' as well as the competency to consistently deliver on your commitments to self and others. I prefer 'invested' to 'involved', however the meaning is the same as Sieler's.

Rachel Botsman, a world leading authority on trust, and author of *Who Can You Trust?*, talks about the importance of 'consistency' as being core to trust in both the domains of 'being' and 'doing'. Having read some of her work on this and assessing her to be a world leader in contemporary thinking on trust, I have added it into this second edition.

Charles Feltman, Founder and Owner of Insight Coaching and author of *The Thin Book of Trust*, shared on a podcast with Brené

Brown that trust is "choosing to risk making something you value vulnerable to another person's actions". Linked to this is you appropriately sharing your vulnerability with others you want to trust and whom you want to trust you. Ashkan Tashvir, Founder of the Being Framework and author of both *Human Being* and *Being*, writes, "when someone voluntarily acknowledges their vulnerabilities, it demonstrates their strength and authenticity". I now feel that vulnerability is core to an assessment of trust in the domain of 'being', and as such have added this into this second edition too.

Given these additions, and my distinction later in the book of 'way of being' and way of doing', I am arguing that there are 'Seven Assessments of Trust' (as shown below), not Sieler's four, that are split as follows: three in the domain of being, three in the domain of doing and one, 'consistently', that envelopes both.

The Seven Assessments of Trust

Think of these 'Assessments of Trust' in these two ways:

1. **Do I trust you?** – Are you invested in me and my concerns? Are you sincere in that investment? Are you being vulnerable and open to being vulnerable to my actions? Are you reliable? Do you deliver on your commitments? Do you have the competency to deliver on your commitments? Do you have the capacity to deliver on your commitments? Do you do all this consistently?

2. **Am I trustworthy?** – Am I invested in you and your concerns? Am I sincere in that investment? Am I being vulnerable and open to being vulnerable to your actions? Am I reliable? Do I deliver on my commitments? Do I have the competency to deliver on my commitments? Do I have the capacity to deliver on my commitments? Do I do all this consistently?

By asking these 16 questions both of self, and about another, you will be mitigating the risk of whether to trust this person (and yourself) before going into a relationship, making an offer or making a request of someone to do something for you.

There is some similarity here with the 'equation of trust', created by Charles H. Green – author, speaker and world expert on trust-based relationships and sales in complex businesses – and David H. Maister – who, prior to his retirement in 2009, was widely acknowledged as one of the world's leading authorities on the management of professional service firms – in their book *The Trusted Advisor* (2002). Their Trust Equation uses four variables to measure trustworthiness. These four variables are: Credibility+Reliability+Intimacy 'divided by' Self-Orientation. It is a way of explaining and visualising trust that has been used extensively in business since 2002.

In my view, trust is ultimately when both parties in a relationship deliver on their commitments consistently, and/or when you deliver on your commitments consistently that you make to yourself. If this element fails, we lose trust in ourselves and in others, and others lose their trust in you.

However, it's so much deeper than this, as demonstrated further on in this book and in my model that creates a New Ordering of Trust. As humans, we need order to function and make sense of things. I hope my model creates a New Order for you to see how trust is omnipresent in your life and in society at large.

I say trust is a choice, and I base this on my coaching (and my life) framework of Observe|Choose|Act. If you can be an observer of yourself (and your environment) you will open yourself up to more choice, or possibilities, from where you can then take action. In the case of trust, if you are able to observe how you trust yourself, how you trust others and how they trust you, that will lead to greater choices and possibilities of what action you take to build trust, both in yourself and in those around you.

Ask yourself this question: how is this notion of trust and what I'm reading now going to help me in my day job? When you understand that trust is ever-present, it will ensure you see it as something which is important and therefore something to focus on, in order for you to deliver results as a leader and have a more fulfilling life.

You might also be asking yourself why you need historical evidence of trust. Well, by sharing with you how it's been ever present in history, it gives evidence to my assessment that it is a basis of evolution of human society.

So why do you need to know about this thing called Ontology? It's the basis of my model, a New Ordering of Trust. By sharing with you its genesis, it gives credence to its existence as a philosophy that can be used in life in general, and trust in particular.

If you want to read more on the history or meaning of trust or about Ontology, please research them to gain a deeper understanding. I won't be going too much deeper into the history and philosophy of Ontology other than what I've already provided to you here. If you want to contact me and find out more, my details are at the end of the book and all my references are provided at the end of the book too.

Trust and consistently delivering on commitments

Delivering on your commitments consistently can be both to yourself and to someone else. To truly deliver on your commitments consistently, it must come from within you – from your heart and not from your head. When it comes from your heart, you're in acceptance of, or at peace, with what is.

In this context a commitment is simply (not simple to do) doing what you say you are going to do, both to yourself and for others. To be an effective leader and an authentic human, you have to consistently deliver on your commitments. Your brand and your character are judged by others on how you deliver on this. To be at peace with yourself, you must be both sincere and value where others come from and their stories, as well as them as human beings.

When I joined a leading retailer in Australia to run their logistics in 2011, I now feel and know that I didn't consistently deliver on my commitments that I made to the leaders of that organisation. I was too busy thinking about my career in that organisation instead of being focused on the outcomes that I was expected to deliver. They had every right to expect I would consistently deliver on the commitments that I made. I use the 'first person' here, as it is about my commitments, however, clearly, I couldn't have done anything without the team. I was expected to reduce the distribution costs as a percentage of sales, and the cost per carton of a carton through the distribution network – which I did. However, I know that I didn't deliver to the level that was expected by the leadership team and committed to by me. I also made the commitment to build on, and move forward, the culture of high performance and safety in logistics. Again, I made changes, but not to the level that was required by the board and the leaders of that organisation.

I worked extremely hard, under the extreme pressure of expectations. At a particular time of crisis, I did deliver on my commitments and was recognised for it. However, in the nearly two years I was there, I don't feel I fully delivered on what I committed to others. I wasn't at peace with myself, or trusting myself, as I was delivering for myself, and this showed in the delivery of my commitments. My reputation and brand were judged accordingly. I was simply too ambitious, driven by ego and already thinking about the next opportunity – a place in the Executive running the whole supply chain function.

I'm telling this story to show that by not understanding trust and by not understanding myself fully at the time, it affected the consistent delivery of my commitments – and therefore my brand and reputation.

Conversely, when I joined a leading Australian manufacturer to run their logistics and planning in 2006, I delivered on my commitment to improve the logistics and planning costs and service levels, made to the CEO when he brought me from the UK to join his leadership team. My career grew, and I was asked to take on more and more responsibility in my time there. In those four years, I was more at peace with myself and was sincere in my commitment to deliver for others, more than myself.

Later in this book, I'll unpack a methodology, a model, and a New Ordering of Trust that allows you to become the person who consistently delivers on your commitments, both to self and others.

On a more personal basis, this book is about sharing commitments made to myself and not keeping them. Those commitments came from my head and not my heart. These failed commitments are shown in my stories, which are my assessments, or interpretations, of the situations. I will cover the notion of stories and their importance to us, and to trust, in the next chapter.

Head vs heart

Up until three years ago, I had always made personal commitments to put my family first as the 'right thing to do'. However, at times my commitments have come from my head and not my heart. Part of my head was my ego and believing that by delivering on my goals that would take care of my family. This has led me to failing at times in my commitment to my family and others. Who was I really invested in? Me or my family and my relationships? If you can touch your heart, you will find the answer to that. I have. For this, I apologise to those who I've let down both on a personal relationship basis outside of work and a work relationship basis when I've made commitments to them. You can be 'successful' and still get it wrong, however you define success. I have, at times, 'got it wrong'.

I've seen many smart people make similar mistakes. I may not claim to be super smart myself, but I've seen many smart people do what I've done – not always being invested in the other person or consistently delivering on their commitments, with an erosion of trust being the outcome.

You may be thinking, "Surely trust is more than consistently delivering on a commitment and being invested in another?" It is, and I'll share that with you throughout this book. However, the ultimate manifestation of it is whether or not you are vulnerable and open to being vulnerable to another's actions, invested in another's concerns, are sincere in this, and consistently deliver on your commitments. Where this commitment comes from is key – your head or your heart. I believe true trust in self is when it comes from the heart or your *hara*. In Japanese culture your *hara* is your true centre and the core of your being, where your true knowing lies. Physiologically the *hara* is actually just below the belly. Thank you to my friend Tessa Van Keeken, for giving me this knowledge through her reiki meditation practices.

Is it only your heart or is it intuition? In this chapter, it's okay for you to see intuition and heart as the same. Here when I refer to 'heart', I'm referring to your physiology below the neck – your nervous system below the neck (as the brain is a part of your nervous system).

When have you not been vulnerable and vulnerable to another's actions? Not been invested in another? Or not consistently delivered on your commitments? Where did the commitment that you made come from? Was it from your head or from your heart? Conversely, when did you allow yourself to be vulnerable and vulnerable to the actions of another, sincerely invest in another and consistently deliver on your commitments? Can you think about where those commitments came from? Did they come from your head or from your heart?

Making the distinction between your head and your heart is exceedingly difficult. As you read this, feel your emotion, or

What is trust and why does it matter?

what energy is flowing in you right now. What sensations do you notice in your body as you read this? This is you starting to connect with your heart and your physiology 'below the neck'.

Trust in a leader

You need trust for others to follow you or to *choose* to follow you as a leader. Unless people choose to follow you because it takes care of their concerns, you are not truly a leader and your leadership will fail. Being vulnerable, invested in the other and delivering consistently on your commitments underpins this foundation of trust. Are you taking care of their concerns and providing them with a pathway to follow you?

I'd like to share with you the views of three other leading contemporary writers on leadership and trust, as well as a personal story about the importance of being a great leader where others choose to follow you due to their trust in you.

Robert Hurley, in his 2006 *Harvard Business Review* article 'The Decision to Trust', shares that "roughly half of all managers don't trust their leaders". His research shows that the environments with low trust are described by those he has surveyed as "stressful, threatening, divisive, unproductive and tense". These are clearly not environments conducive to high-quality work or outstanding results, or fun places to spend most of your working day in.

Hurley has "developed a model that can be used to predict whether an individual will choose to trust or distrust another in a given situation". The importance of being armed with this knowledge, he says, is that those leaders "took concrete steps that made it easier for others to place confidence in them". I am not going into Hurley's model. Whatever model you choose to use, his, mine or someone else's, the point is, as a leader you need to take 'concrete steps' for others to place confidence in you. I hope my model and New Ordering of Trust supports you in doing that.

One of the foremost contemporary writers in the space of trust is Stephen M.R. Covey with his books *The Speed of Trust* (2006) and *Smart Trust* (2011). He is the son of Stephen R. Covey, best-selling author of *The 7 Habits of Highly Effective People*.

For me, his work builds on the work of Hurley, with regards to a toxic culture, and then drives it home in terms of value or return on investment. In his video on his Franklin Covey website 'speed of trust' he talks about the "The Speed of Trust Multiplier" as a formula (Strategy × Execution) × Trust = Result.

His teaching is that trust always affects these two outcomes of speed and cost – pretty vital to any leaders' armoury. When trust goes down, speed will also go down and costs will go up. When trust goes up, speed will also go up and costs will go down. This is illustrated by Ameet Ranadive, an entrepreneur, on medium.com 'the four corners of trust', as shared here.

The speed of trust

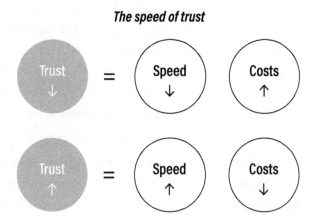

In the relationship of trust to leadership, Prudy Gourguechon, a leading contributor on leadership strategy for forbes.com, wrote in the 2018 *Forbes* article 'Why Inspiring Trust And Trusting Others Are Essential Leadership Capacities' that "the capacity for trust – both to trust others and to inspire trust – is a fundamental character trait every leader with great responsibility must have." I couldn't agree more.

Finally, storytelling author Gabrielle Dolan sums this up perfectly in her 2019 book *Real Communication*: "Without trust, we don't make decisions as quickly, or we take more time to double check information ... If we don't trust our partners, we spend a lot of time thinking and expecting the worst ... As a leader if your people don't trust you, they will not follow you. And if you look over your shoulder and no one is following you, guess what? You may have the title of leader, but you are not a leader. The title is all you have." I have no qualms with that.

In 2007, a year after coming to Australia, I was asked to take on the extra responsibility for group safety by the CEO of National Foods (now part of Bega). I'd never led safety for a multibillion-dollar organisation, and certainly not in an agricultural and fast-moving consumer goods company (FMCG). I found the courage to take up the opportunity offered, was vulnerable and curious to learn from the best in class externally to the organisation, shared those learnings with others and challenged the beliefs in the organisation that safety was only a manufacturing issue – when statistically, at that time, our worst performing function for injuries was in-the-field sales.

By trusting my heart and being courageous and vulnerable as a learner, at the end of this journey I knew I had invested myself in others' concerns, at times been vulnerable to their actions, and consistently delivered on my commitments. I was trusted by my CEO, colleagues, safety committees around the country, and the business as a whole, to lead a culture of safety improvement. More people went home uninjured every day than was the case before we embarked on this journey, and the trust that the people had in the leaders of the organisation to care for their safety grew exponentially, as was verified in the surveys taken during that time. There are people who were in that organisation who still talk about that time in their lives to this day. Clearly, I am one of them!

I would like to thank my two safety colleagues David Scott and David Hopkins, world-leading safety consultant Ben Wilson, my CEO Ashley Waugh, my leadership team colleagues, all the leaders in the business, and those working every day in the business, for wholeheartedly buying into the Destination Zero vision and executing the strategy collectively. It was a team effort, regardless of my role as the leader of it.

If people choose not to follow me, will I fail as a leader? Yes, ultimately. You may deliver acceptable results for your organisation, your stakeholders, and your board in the short to medium term, but is that really all leadership is about? I don't think so. Also, are those results sustainable in the long term if people choose not to follow you?

You may also be asking, "Do I have to always be vulnerable and vulnerable to others' actions, invested in another person's concerns and consistently deliver on my commitments to be trusted as a person and as a leader?" Yes, you do. Have you ever felt trusted by your team, colleagues, boss, or those deeper in the organisation when you know you haven't been vulnerable, invested yourself in another's concerns and consistently delivered on your commitments? I don't think so.

There may have been a time when you delivered despite not being trusted. However, did that last long? Or was it a particular success which was surrounded by other times where you didn't feel trusted or able to consistently deliver on your commitments?

Ask yourself: when have I felt most trusted by those around me? What is the relationship to those times and being vulnerable, as well as vulnerable to their actions, invested in another's concerns while consistently delivering on my commitments, either to myself or to others?

It's difficult to separate delivering results in the field of business to feeling trusted. Reflect on the conversations that you may have had at the time and use them as grounds for whether or not you were trusted, or whether you delivered despite not being trusted. It may be the lack of conversations you had at the time that might be the tell-tale for you.

With trust, your life is more fulfilled

Life is to be enjoyed, if possible, and for you to leave a mark or a legacy in some way – even if your legacy is that you were a good person and others felt richer for having been in your presence. Not a bad one to have, I may say.

You don't have to be a Beethoven, Einstein, Washington, Brunel, Churchill, Gandhi, Mother Teresa, or others who've made an imprint in history as a legacy. Without trusting yourself, you trusting others, and others trusting you, leaving a legacy will be more difficult, if not impossible. You will probably be remembered more for your ego or self-fulfilment than a true legacy.

Trust is a core element to finding peace and enjoyment of life. If you can find peace and enjoy life, even in times of hardship, then life can be more fulfilling and meaningful. By having joy, fulfilment and meaning in your life, you're more likely to trust yourself, trust others and be trusted by others – all of which is part of being the most effective leader that you want to be.

My life is richer now than ever before because I've learned to trust myself from below my neck – my heart, my *hara*, my nervous system, my physiology, my emotions, and moods. Instead of living in the stories in my head about what success is, I listen to my energy flow – moods and emotions – and I sense in my body how to guide myself to having more fulfilment in my life.

By doing this, I live more for others and less for myself, which means that I'm a better husband, father, son, brother, coach, and leader in my professional field. I am more trusted and trust myself more.

Think of Simba in *The Lion King* – let down by his uncle, Scar, and made to believe in his head that he couldn't be trusted by his pride because he had killed his father. A period in exile where he gets in touch with himself at a deeper level, with the help of others. He comes back, fights for what he left and begins a new journey as the leader of the pride. He is fulfilled, trusts himself, trusts others and is trusted by his pride. I feel that I am living this Simba story. You've got to love Disney for providing a metaphor to that narrative!

Finally, think of Mahatma Gandhi who, through fulfilment and meaning in life, was trusted by millions of his kinfolk to deliver Indian independence on 15 August 1947. Even though he was "a difficult mentor and alienated the public then as now", according to *National Geographic Magazine* in July 2015. He has left an enduring legacy, a legacy that was created by having a more fulfilled life because of others trusting him and choosing to follow him.

So, you're telling me I have to be Simba and go into exile, or Gandhi with his deep beliefs to be fulfilled and trusted as a person or leader? No. However, by finding trust in yourself below the neck, you're more likely to be fulfilled, trust yourself, trust others and be trusted by others.

What fulfils you?

What fulfils you? What is your purpose? How do you define (or possibly redefine) success? By answering these questions and potentially taking action on them, you may find you trust yourself and your intuition more. You may trust others and be trusted by others more as you are living a life of fulfilment and legacy, rather than a life of ego and external success.

Asking yourself what fulfils you is not something you do every day. Here are some questions that may help you answer this question from different perspectives:

- What is my purpose?
- What are my values, and what value(s) do I refuse to compromise?
- What fulfills me?
- What do I find joy in?
- Can I find *one word* that is the essence of me?
- What *really* matters to me in life? And how can I take care of these core matters? (I call these 'concerns' in my Coaching Practice, which will now be used throughout this book.)
- How do I define success in my life?

- Related to your job – what matters to you personally and professionally in a role?

- How can you integrate your personal and your professional life into one?

Having done this, I know and feel that my *one word* is 'beacon', and my purpose is 'to be a beacon for others'.

A great book around Purpose is *Ikigai, The Japanese Secret to a Long and Happy Life* by Hector Garcia and Francesc Miralles (2016). I won't be going into any more detail on this subject here, so that might support you to go deeper into this domain of self.

Don't try to balance your home and work life – integrate them. If you're integrating, you're coming from within. It's a holistic way of viewing your life. If you're balancing them, you're outside of yourself and you are looking at it in a binary way.

Look at the illustration below to see the difference between the binary scales of balance and the integrated circle of life.

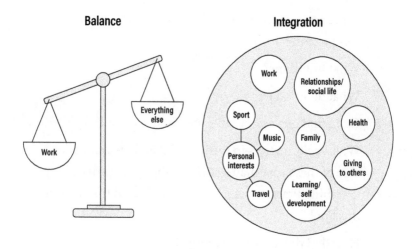

The size of the inner circles in the illustration on the right may expand and contract depending on how they ebb and flow in importance in your life. Other circles may come in, as some leave. These inner circles that represent what matters to you in your life are never outside the circle, they are always inside, as there is only one you. Life is not binary, that is for sure!

Conclusion

You've learned the importance of trust in human and societal evolution, and the Ontological context of my model and New Ordering of Trust, the detail of which I share in chapter three.

Ultimately, trust is about being vulnerable and being vulnerable to the action of another, investing yourself in another's concerns, being sincere in that, and consistently delivering on your commitments to yourself and others, from your heart. Trust is essential to leadership, to others choosing to follow you, to leading a fulfilling life and leaving a legacy.

The main barrier may be allowing yourself to go deeper into this topic – I hope the following chapters will help you do this.

I hope that the deeper meaning of trust that I will share in this book pervades your whole 'Way of Being'.

Practical application

Take time to reflect and do some of the actions and suggestions outlined in this chapter before moving on to chapter two.

I hope you'll reflect on the importance of trust in everything that you do, in your relationships and in your conversations with others – and how it affects your life being fulfilled or not.

What's coming up?

- I'll share with you some more personal stories of trust so you can get to know me a bit more.

- I will share how living in your stories directly affects how you understand trust, how you lead and how it affects your relationships with other people.

Two

Stories and trust

We live in our stories and this directly affects how we understand trust and how we understand our relationships with other people. These stories are core to our 'way of being'.

A story is the way that we interpret the facts of our experiences. The way we understand trust is built, in part, from the stories we live in. You may have come across the notion of 'Origin Stories' when reading about comic book characters or famous people. This is the theme of this chapter, however in this case it is related to you, how you trust yourself and why you may or may not trust others.

Your stories come from your culture, your family, and your lived experience.

To understand your stories and how they impact your leadership, you must understand the distinction between assessments (beliefs) and assertions (facts).

I'm going to share with you my personal story – from childhood to starting work – from the position of assessments (beliefs) vs assertions (facts), and also share some personal leadership experiences of trust to expand on this distinction.

When you can make these distinctions and understand the notion of 'living in your stories', it will help you make sense of how you think, how you see the world and why you may (or may not) trust someone or something.

If you can see your life's journey as a story or a series of stories, it will help you see things differently and give you new perspectives to support your life and leadership approach. Bill Ash, in his book *Redesigning Conversations* (2021), calls these stories our "scripts" that you may prefer to use.

By reading some of my stories, I hope it will help you look into yours and possibly choose to re-narrate them, to serve you better. If you choose not to learn from your stories, you're probably not open to learning and seeing new possibilities for action as a leader. If you are not a learner, you are not a leader. Yes, those two statements are meant to challenge you.

Where your stories come from

Your stories come from three domains of reflection – your culture, your family, and your lived experience. How you make sense of your stories is to distinguish between what is the fact in the story (the assertion), and what is the belief or narrative you are holding about the story (the assessment).

By understanding your stories or the narratives that you live with and have lived with, it helps you make sense of them. This, in turn, helps you understand more about the basis of trust, who you trust, what you trust and how you trust yourself.

Part of making sense of this is to drill into the fact in the story and the belief or the narrative. By doing this, you will see that a lot of what you believe to be true are a number of assessments (beliefs) bound together in a narrative, in which the facts are somewhat buried. If you don't break them down and reflect on them, you will live in the same narrative that you've always done. You won't be open to learning and you won't see possibilities in the current moment, as your story of that particular issue may hold you back.

Stories Venn diagram

Adapted from Alan Sieler, *Coaching to the Human Soul, volume one*

As you can see, the Venn diagram shows that our stories are in three domains – our culture, our family, and our lived experience.

The first circle is the culture. I don't know where you come from with regard to your culture. My culture is based on a Western culture. I was born in the UK and follow a Western belief system. Unless I actively choose to 'wipe' my culture there is nothing I can do about that.

To a degree, the culture that I was born into will have affected the family environment that I've grown up in, which is the second circle. There will be a certain set of beliefs and norms in Western/ UK culture that will be endemic in part of my family upbringing. If you are from the same culture at birth as me, we will share similar narratives. It is in our family experiences that we will start to diversify. I'll share later about my family experience, which may be somewhat divergent to yours. It is that family experience that is the start of the journey of how you see, and make meaning of, the world.

The final circle is my and your lived experience. This is where the divergence between me as the author and you as the reader will start to widen even further. We may share similar experiences as leaders of organisations or business units, however there will be different life experiences, and the communities/organisations that we have lived in/been a part of will provide us with different beliefs and standards, that we now live our lives by.

The intersection of all three circles is 'your story'.

In this chronological view of the circles, from culture to family to lived experience, I see a relationship to Kegan's adult stages of development in his book *In Over Our Heads*, where he talks about the five developmental stages/orders of mind, from 'impulsive mind' through to the 'self-transforming mind'. For me, his chronology of development relates to how we observe our stories, from the lens of the three circles. Initially we only have the culture we are born into as the reference point, which then expands into our family experience. This shift in our internal narrative runs in parallel to us shifting through the formative stages of development ('impulsive'/'instrumental'). As we grow older, in the lived experience circle, we shift from a 'socialised mind' through a 'self-authoring mind' and ultimately to a 'self-transforming mind' (if we are able to shift our self-learning far enough to achieve that state).

You might see that over time the first two circles effectively decrease in size relatively, as you lean more into learning from your lived experience and less from your family experience and the culture you were born into. However, if you feel this is not the case, what are you not observing and learning from in your current lived experience? Are you over-relying on your culture and family experience in your inner narrative and storytelling?

That is a way to make sense of the stories that you tell yourself and that you live in every day.

Think of the culture you were born into, think of your family experience, and then think of your lived experience. Think of the relativity of the size of the circles of the stories that you are telling yourself. This might help you understand how you can now write the stories that you are living in.

Assessments and assertions

I now want to introduce the distinction between assessments (beliefs) and assertions (facts). Assertions are facts that you can verify, or society can verify. Society is the organisation you work in or the society you're a part of. Assessments are our beliefs. Let me tell you, we can get these two very mixed up!

I went to this school from this date to that date. I live at this address, which is _____. It is 16 degrees today. Scotland last won a Grand Slam in rugby in 1990. The Melbourne Rebels have never made the Super 15 final playoffs. (As I shared with you in the introduction, you can tell from this that one of my passions is rugby!) Those are facts that you can look at in your own life and see them as such – or assertions.

Assessments are narratives or beliefs that we overlay onto the facts. I went to this school and it was a great experience. I live in this house and it is on a nice street in a nice suburb. It is hot today. Scotland has been unlucky in not winning a Grand Slam since 1990. The Melbourne Rebels are lucky to still be in the Super Rugby competition. All of these are assessments that I am making, and you can challenge them with your own assessments.

Too often, we see our assessments as facts – especially as leaders. Unfortunately, the way you present them in language to yourself, and to others, can influence how you lead and what others hear you say.

How often have you said, "that result is not acceptable", or "that role must have these competencies and experiences", in such a way that your listener hears it as a fact? It is an assessment against a criterion that you have in your head or possibly against a standard that you have both agreed to. However, it is not a fact or an assertion, it is an assessment. The fact is your direct report's business unit missed EBITDA by X dollars against the plan, or that person did not deliver your report on Friday – which they committed to. The assessment is you saying that the result is not acceptable.

The distinctions of the words assessments and assertions that I choose to use are based on the words of Fernando Flores, referred to in conversationsforaction.com.

ICF accredited and NeuroLeadership Group and Presence Based coach Ronni Hendel-Giller wrote in November 2016 on *Actionableblog* when talking about Flores, that when "we make statements, they are primarily either assertions or assessments. Assertions can be proven to be true or false. Assessments are not absolutely true or false but are a contextual or relative statement – or an opinion." I believe this is a particularly good explanation of the difference between the two.

We even learned this distinction in primary school. On reviewing a level 5 lesson plan for eight to nine year olds by *Victoria Walks* in Australia, I found that the key learning outcomes were "students will be able to identify an assertion, challenge an assertion, temper an assertion, write an informative piece about assertions."

Many of us are taught these distinctions at an early age, possibly at school or by our parents. However, we seem to forget them or choose to ignore them and simply believe our stories to be true or 'the truth'.

Let me bring assessments (beliefs) and assertions (facts) together on a personal basis.

I was born in 1965 in the swinging 1960s UK (already an asser-tion and assessment made in ten words!). There's nothing I can do about that. I wasn't born into an Asian culture, I wasn't born into a Middle Eastern culture, I wasn't born into any other type of culture. I was born into a Western culture with narratives and beliefs stemming from World War II and the liberating times of the 1960s. I was born into a Catholic, Scottish, and Irish family where the standards were extremely high. There was a strong work ethic and a Monty-Pythonesque view of what good looks like in terms of hierarchy in society and what success looks like in life. For me, that was going to school, doing the best I could at school, going to university, getting a job, providing for my family, being a leader – and all the other standards and beliefs that come with that through my family experience.

In my childhood, I lived in England and Scotland before we moved to Australia when I was eight. After 12 months in Australia, my brother and I went to a boarding school in England (The Oratory School), where my grandfather was Deputy Head. He was also our English teacher – not many of you will have been taught by your grandad! My parents moved from Australia to Indonesia, to Singapore, to India, to Israel, to Greece, to Spain, and finally to Holland. Every summer was spent somewhere different in the world, and every Christmas we spent at our home in Braemar, in the Highlands of Scotland. Easter was sometimes in Scotland and sometimes where my parents were living at the time. In summary, we lived around the world with a home in Scotland. It is at this juncture I would like to thank my mother for always creating a loving home environment, wherever we were living around the world, at times moving within 12 months, due to my father's work in the oil industry. Quite an achievement and legacy.

As shared with you, I went to the Oratory School, an English Catholic boarding school, from 1975 to 1984. I went to the University of Aberdeen from 1984 to 1988, graduating with an MA honours degree in political studies. These are assertions (facts).

I'm a Scot with an Irish name and an English accent, who is an Aussie too. As a passionate Scot, I had to go to a Scottish university to finish my education. My English accent is the chip on my shoulder! That is the story I live with to this day, which is an assessment (a belief).

This will inevitably create stories of how I see the world, with this family environment and lived experience. In terms of culture, there is self-reliance in a very privileged UK boarding school education from the age of nine, with home being the Highlands of Scotland and the experience of all these countries as a youngster.

The lived experience continues through my first job after leaving university, where I joined a division of a business my father worked for. He worked for Christian Salvesen, which at the time was a privately owned Scottish multinational business with operations in shipping, oil exploration and services, logistics, house building and power generation. That is what took us around the world. I joined that organisation in 1988 on their management training scheme in their logistics business, after a summer working in that company in the US in 1987. Because my father was a senior leader in the organisation, I felt I had to be especially successful there in my own right. In my early career in that business, I was always Peter O'Malley's son. The day that somebody said to my dad, "You're Conor O'Malley's father," meant I had arrived, and that was success for me!

These are my stories and they're littered with both assertions (facts) and assessments (narratives/beliefs). I will leave it to you to work out which are which.

Surely one person's view of an assessment can be another person's view of an assertion? Not really, however I accept it can be a grey area, without forensic examination.

The safest way to make the distinction is to ask, "Can I verify my assessment with facts?" If not, it is an assessment.

Is it in any way grey? In most places, there is no grey. However, if you want to go to a deeper existential philosophical view, and ask "Is the chair that you're sitting on really a chair?" or "Are Celsius and Fahrenheit the only ways to measure temperature?", or into the depths of early existentialism, when Sartre posed a question in his book *La Nausee*, written in 1938, where Roquentin questions if a tram seat is really a seat or actually a dead donkey, that is taking the meaning of assessment and an assertion too far for this book!

Think of your own life in the context of the Venn diagram. What meaning do you make of it? You could go through this chapter and work out which parts in my story are assessments and assertions, using a highlighter pen. I know this might ruin your book, but it might help you make sense of my story from this distinction.

Finally, you can use a six-stage approach to 'ground your assessment' to see if something you believe is 'true'.

Here's the approach asking yourself six questions that you can use at any time, both from a leadership perspective and a self-questioning perspective:

1. **"For the sake of what?"** For the sake of what future action am I making this assessment? In other words, is it really important to go to the next four stages? For example, "I don't like vanilla ice cream" – assertion or assessment? Who cares? Make up your mind and move on. If you can't do it quickly and it has an impact on a future action that matters to you, then go to the next stage.

2. **"In what domain am I making this assessment?"** For example, you may say to yourself and others that John is lazy. Is that a fact or is that a belief? Is John only lazy at work or is he lazy all the time? He may be highly active and far from lazy in the community. It may only be at work that he's lazy. Are you saying actually it is in the domain of work that he is lazy? Is he really lazy?

3. **"To what standard?"** Staying with the example of John being lazy at work, to what standard are you holding him to be lazy? Your standard? The standard that is acceptable in your workplace? Look at your own standards of lazy, in this case, first. Are they fair? Are they reasonable? Are they appropriate? What is the standard of the environment

you are leading or operating in? How does your standard compare to this? This notion of a 'standard' is extremely broad; it is basically to a standard that you/your work environment/your society find acceptable, in any domain.

4. **"What is the evidence for your assessment?"** What is the evidence for John being lazy at work?

5. **"What is the evidence against your assessment?"** What is the evidence against John being lazy at work?

6. **"Should you re-assess your initial assessment?"** Use what you have learned in the previous five stages to go back to your initial assessment and re-assess it. Was it 'true'?

The first five stages of this model are outlined by Alan Sieler in his book *Coaching to the Human Soul* volume one. The sixth stage was suggested to me by a client who said, "so the sixth stage is re-assessing your assessment, using the previous five stages". Very insightful, so I have included it in this second edition as a sixth stage.

By going through this process, you can come to a much more informed view about the assessment (belief) you are making or holding and how it is helping or hindering you.

You can get caught up in your stories and not see them for what they are. Try and break yours down by seeing where they come from using the Venn diagram. Also try to make some distinctions between assessments (beliefs) and assertions (facts).

My deeper stories of assessments and assertions

I'm including more of my personal story of assessments and assertions here to help you make meaning of yours and tell you more about myself and my way of thinking.

By addressing this story further, it embeds the notion of how we live in our stories and how that relates to our view of trust. By not addressing this, the point may not be made and the importance of stories to the rest of the book could be lost.

I lived in a story of 'success in life' until five years ago. My story used to be that, unless I was CEO of a multimillion- or multibillion-dollar organisation, I wasn't successful. This story drove me to make the choices that I made both personally and professionally. It was self-limiting and, at times, destructive. I've since re-narrated that story to one that is not self-limiting. For me, now, success is believing – and feeling – that I am a 'Beacon for others'. I'm living in service of others, and it is they who will determine if I'm a beacon for them or not. However, at a more existential level, I also have my own internal beacon and it's my responsibility to nurture that beacon to be a beacon for myself.

Where did this self-limiting belief of 'having to be a CEO' stem from? As you know, I went to the Oratory School between 1975 and 1984 and to the University of Aberdeen from 1984 to 1988. What I haven't shared is that I was captain of the school and captain of the rugby team. Prior to university, I got a scholarship to become an officer in the British army and go to Sandhurst, the British army officer training school. I resigned from Sandhurst on the day I received my probationary commission as a second lieutenant. In my second year at university, I played club rugby rather than continue to play for my university. These are all facts in my early life – assertions.

The stories I now know I was living in are that I 'had' to be captain of the school and captain of rugby to be 'successful', that I didn't get into the University of Edinburgh because I didn't get the grades – I wasn't academically strong, therefore I had to go to the University of Aberdeen. That I decided not to take up my commission because my commitment to the army in university would affect my chance of playing rugby for Scotland. I believed, at the age of 18, that when I could first leave the army at the age of 25, that my career would be more advanced if I had gone into industry. I also believed that playing club rugby instead of university rugby was my best chance of playing provincial rugby, which was the main pathway to playing for Scotland in those days – which was my only standard of success as a rugby player.

These are stories I told myself.

However, the reality is that I actually worked a lot harder in my political studies A-level than my geography A-level, which I didn't like to admit. (A-levels are the university entry exams in the UK.) The grade that I needed to get into Edinburgh was in the subject that I didn't work awfully hard in.

The reality is that I only took the army scholarship to prove I could attain it. I didn't really want to be an army officer, I aimed for the 'best the army could offer an 18-year-old' as a notch on my belt of 'success'. Having been given the chance to stay, as I passed all that was required, I left because it was not an environment for me.

As for rugby, the reality is I did play provincial under-21 rugby and was selected for the trials in the senior provincial team while at university. However, I wasn't selected to represent the senior provincial side after those trials. Therefore, I wasn't good enough to play at that level or for Scotland.

Another reality is that I was awarded the highest sporting honour that the school could bestow in rugby, the 'silver cap'. My self-limiting story is that when my father came to see me play, I never played very well and told myself it was because he was watching me. However, I obviously did play well, given the honour bestowed on me in this sport. The story I was telling myself was based on the standards that I felt my father was setting for me and based on my childhood and what standards I thought were good standards. I held myself to a standard that was not necessarily fair and right, simply because my father was watching me. What son does not concern himself with what he believes his father thinks? I choose now to believe that I was good at rugby. It is a fact (an assertion) that my first game in every club that I have joined, from leaving school to giving up rugby as a 40-year-old in Australia, has been in the club's 1st xv (there was only one 'Vets' team in my club in Melbourne, so I guess that counts as a 1st xv!). The assessment is, I just was not good enough for the ambition I had. It is at this stage of the book I would like to thank my great friend now, and mentor at the time, Paul Keddie, who was my rugby coach, for his counsel in my school days and his (and his wife Dawn's) friendship to this very day.

This is re-narrating my stories to be less self-limiting and see more of others' perspectives rather than looking at only my own. A term you may prefer to use is "re-authoring your scripts", as Bill Ash does in his book *Redesigning Conversations* (2021).

You may be thinking that I see my stories through a 'negative' lens and that's possibly true. That's why I've chosen to re-narrate my stories to see more 'positives' in them. I put these two words in quote marks because they are neither positive nor negative. I ask you to see that they either serve you well or less well, not in a binary meaning of good/bad or positive/negative. If you're potentially thinking of your stories through a lens where those stories don't serve you well, look at them and re-narrate them to see what assertions or assessments you can draw from them that *do* serve you well, and then see what you can learn from them.

Practical application

Think of your childhood stories, as I've done above. Write them out. And this time, instead of highlighting the assessments (beliefs) and assertions (facts) of my stories, look at your own. What are the assessments (beliefs) and what are the assertions (facts)? It's difficult and takes a bit of practice but keep looking at the facts. The rest are interpretations of the facts and the story that surrounds them – ask yourself, "How are these stories serving me?"

If you keep your stories as constructions in your mind you will miss seeing possibilities and it can be exhausting living in them. You can free yourself from being attached to these narratives, if you see them for what they are – stories that are full of assessments based on your culture, family and lived experience.

Trust, listening and being a learner

I'm now going deeper into my leadership stories so you can get to know me more as an adult and hopefully evoke your own adult stories in order to separate the assessments (beliefs) and the assertions (facts) in that domain.

This will lead to you understanding yourself better, which will then potentially lead you to understanding more about who, and what, you do and don't trust.

A key part of a trust is listening and soliciting feedback. If you don't listen or solicit feedback, you may think that you know best. If that is the case, trust is either eroded or not ever-present. If you don't listen and seek feedback, you become the expert in your own mind. It's highly possible that if you don't listen or solicit feedback, you'll be operating from a 'fixed mindset', to coin the phrase from Carol Dweck, "a pioneering researcher in the field of motivation", as shared on her TED talk page.

You will be in opposition to learning and you won't see possibilities, which I'll expand on later in the book. It's so important for leadership at whatever level to have a learner's mind, observe yourself as a learner, and to be able to deal with not knowing and uncertainty.

Having a curious mindset, being open to possibilities and accepting uncertainty is so important to listening and soliciting feedback. The world has never been more uncertain than it is today. We are living in a volatile, uncertain, complex, and ambiguous (VUCA) world. VUCA is a commonly used term in today's language of leadership. Sunnie Giles wrote in the 2018 *Forbes* article 'How VUCA is Reshaping the Business Environment and What it Means to Innovation' that "VUCA is a concept that originated with students at the US Army War College to describe volatility, uncertainty, complexity, and ambiguity of the world after the Cold War. And now, the concept is gaining new relevance to characterise the current environment and the leadership required to navigate it successfully."

This is a core concept to understand as a leader today and to be able to listen and solicit feedback as a leader in today's VUCA world.

In the last stage of my career in the supply chain, as a Chief Operating Officer in third-party logistics, I was not listening to 'the tea leaves' of the culture that I was leading in. I led with a belief of what I thought I was employed to do, however I was not listening to the wider culture of the organisation. I was continually trying to prove myself worthy of becoming the CEO, as part of an agreed succession plan.

As Carol Dweck says in her book *Mindset*, "I've seen so many people with this one consuming goal of proving themselves in the classroom, in their careers, and in their relationships. Every situation calls for confirmation of their intelligence, personality, or character. Every situation is evaluated. Will I succeed or fail? Will I look smart or dumb? Will I be accepted or rejected? Will I feel like a winner or a loser?"

I now see that my Way of Being in this role was still being evaluated by me against my definition of success – being the CEO of a multimillion- or multibillion-dollar organisation. At times I wasn't listening, and I interpreted the feedback that I solicited in a different way.

Carol Dweck's fixed mindset model in her 2016 *Harvard Business Review* article 'What Having a Growth Mindset Really Means' described me perfectly: "we all have our own fixed mindset triggers. When we face challenges, receive criticism, or fare poorly compared with others, we can easily fall into insecurity or defensiveness, a response that inhibits growth. Our work environments too can be full of fixed mindset triggers." At times in my career I was defensive and not open to possibilities or being curious. I was trying to be a learner; however, I was coming more from a fixed mindset than a growth mindset.

This concept of fixed and growth mindsets is often used in the context of listening and being curious, which is essential to building trust. However, there is often a misconception around what a growth mindset actually is. There is no better person to debunk this than Dweck herself, who writes in the same *HBR* article: "People often confuse a growth mindset with being flexible or open-minded or having a positive outlook … My colleagues and I call this a false growth mindset."

Having a growth mindset is about your underlying belief in your ability to learn. Without this inner belief that you are a learner and can always learn, you will be inhibited in your ability to be curious, listen and seek feedback. Trust will be eroded and you will not be an effective leader.

Changing tack a wee bit, people will trust you if you're decisive and take action towards a goal. Decisiveness will drive you to your goal, however without listening to others and soliciting feedback by being a learner and being curious, eventually your decisions will not be questioned, or clarity sought, and people will choose not to follow you.

Practical application

Are you listening and soliciting feedback? Ask yourself, "What evidence have I got for and against this assessment?" Do you have a growth mindset? Are you a learner? Do you ever observe yourself existentially how you fare as a learner? Ask those who you work with, and who work for you, whether you are a listener and a person who solicits feedback. You might have to find the courage to ask and the courage to be vulnerable. You may also encounter lack of honesty by those you lead. Do they trust the intention of your question? Will they answer it sincerely and be invested in you when they answer it? As we will see later, this is core to building trust.

Trust and a lack of experience

In 1994, I moved for the first time in my career, from one leading third-party logistics company to another. Moving from the company where Peter O'Malley was known by many as Conor O'Malley's father to a new company where I wasn't known at all,

I lost my sponsorship and also felt I had to know it all. Perhaps I felt I had to 'fake it till I made it'. I was an unknown quantity, other than my reputation in my role at a competitor.

How do those around you trust you when they don't know you? They might perceive, and you certainly feel, that you're inexperienced. Not having self-confidence and not feeling trusted by those around you can be challenging for a highly visible senior leader. Not trusting yourself can lead to micromanagement and a lack of trust in you by others, which causes frustration both ways.

I made the decision to uphold the dismissal of a union official, or 'shop steward' as they're known in the UK. That lit the tinderbox of the site that I'd been employed to lead after less than four weeks in the job. I was not experienced enough, nor did I have the skills to deal with the industrial dispute that resulted from my decision. The union members took the whole distribution centre out on strike, legally.

I didn't feel trusted by my boss or by those on my leadership team. It was the MD who appointed me and not my direct boss, who actually wanted to appoint his chosen successor in my leadership team to the role. I wasn't able to share my feelings of inexperience and lack of competence. I also didn't delegate effectively, as I believed leadership was all about showing strength and not vulnerability. As Robert Whipple, author of *The Trust Factor*, shares on his website, "Trust and delegation go hand in hand because when you delegate something to another person, you're demonstrating trust that the individual will do what is right... By taking the risk of delegating more tasks, leaders can foster an environment of higher trust." I am not sure that I trusted myself, let alone others, to do what was right. I wish I'd had my Seven Assessments of Trust (see chapter one) in my armoury back then!

Another factor that I didn't see was the environment that I was operating and leading in. Using David Snowden and Mary Boone's 2007 article in the *Harvard Business Review*, 'A Leader's Framework for Decision Making', I could have seen that the environment I was working in was complex and not complicated.

Cynefin Framework

COMPLEX
Probe
Sense
Respond

Emergent practice

COMPLICATED
Sense
Analyse
Respond

Good practice

Disorder

CHAOS
Act
Sense
Respond

Novel practice

SIMPLE
Sense
Categorise
Respond

Best practice

Cynefin Framework based on Snowden/Boone 2007 *HBR* article

I sometimes introduce this model to leaders I coach, which you may find useful. I learned this from Carlos Schäfer, a colleague on Julie Birtles' leadership training programme – thanks Carlos. Cynefin is the Welsh word for 'habitat'. By looking at the four quadrants of chaos, complex, complicated, and simple, you can observe the environment that you are both operating and leading in.

When you operate in **Chaos**, there are no patterns. This is where the cause and effect are unknown. The way of operating is to stick a pin in the map and say, "This is where I'm going to make a decision. I may not be right, but any decision is better than no decision." I believe the story of Sergeant Thomas Derrick VC, shows this approach to leadership in battle, where chaos reigned, and 'he stuck a pin in the map'. According to the Australian War Memorial website, on 24 November 1943, Sergeant Derrick was ordered to withdraw from a position in Sattelberg, New Guinea. However, being certain that he and his men could complete their mission, he scaled a cliff and by hurling grenades, single handedly destroyed an enemy post. He continued his scaling and destroyed three more enemy posts as his men came under heavy fire from those posts. The next morning the rest of the battalion captured Sattelberg. For his actions he was awarded the Victoria Cross and part of his citation read – "Undoubtedly Sergeant Derrick's fine leadership and refusal to admit defeat in the face of a seemingly impossible situation resulted in the capture of Sattelberg. His outstanding gallantry, thoroughness and devotion to duty were an inspiration." This is leading in chaos. What is the picture you now have in your mind when you apply that story to your leadership experience today, or in the past?

When you're operating in the **Complex** quadrant, it's exceedingly difficult to see patterns. This is the 'unknown unknowns'. However, by looking at what's going on, you can step above or outside it and see the patterns. By seeing the patterns, you can make sense of the complexity within which you're operating. Think of a time when you see or saw the patterns, but no one else can/could. Is it in the data? Is it in the conversations that people are having? How can you share those patterns that you see with others around you to help them a) see the patterns and b) move into the 'complicated' stage?

Complicated is where the patterns become clearer and the practical side of things comes in. This is the 'known unknowns'. An example would be the Wright brothers' first flight. They saw the patterns in birds and flight, and they took it from a complex environment to a complicated environment, where they created the aeroplane. The aeroplane has gotten more sophisticated, but not a lot has changed, relative to the complexity of flight. Engineers have made the systems and processes and understood it more in this complicated environment. Are you leading in a complicated environment right now?

The fourth quadrant is **Simple** (since 2014 Snowden has renamed this 'Clear'). This is the 'known knowns' where there is 'best practice'. If you stay in the simple box for too long, you don't see the patterns and you end up potentially going back into chaos because you are not a learner (hence the squiggly tail in the framework going from simple to chaos). You reinforce what is best practice and you don't look for the changes that are operating in that environment. Best practice is good; however it can be your undoing.

In my explanations above I have built into Snowden's Cynefin model elements of Martin Broadwell's 'four levels of teaching' model from 1969, which is now commonly referred to as the Conscious Competence Matrix Model.

In this story, as a leader, if I had seen it as complex – which I believe it was – I might have sought support to find the patterns (which were in the history of the site), made a request for help, and delegated more effectively. Clearly, this is me making an assessment (a belief) in hindsight.

Had I observed that, I would have known that I didn't have the experience or competency at that stage to deal with the complex issue. However, the story that I was telling myself was that I was the new kid on the block, and I had to fix this myself and possibly that I had to 'fake it till I made it'. In the final analysis, there was a breakdown in relationships and trust across the board in terms of my ability to deliver on the commitment of getting this distribution centre where it needed to be.

It was a very challenging time, and I ended up taking time off for my mental health and wellbeing. I was asked by the managing director who had recruited me to go back in to lead the site – to 'get back on the horse', as it were. I was supported by my father with his counsel at that difficult time (for which I am forever grateful). I was supported by my wife as we moved in with her sister with our young son (as we were relocating to that area), and by my newly married 'in laws' living in their home. I was supported by the organisation in terms of how to deal technically and legally with the industrial dispute, as well as by more senior management who helped me deal with the retail client. However, after a while, both myself and the organisation felt it was best for me to move to another operation in that business in the same region, as we had moved to a new house by that stage. It was a larger operation where I was '2IC' and had the experience to run that operation. It was a very damaging experience for my self-esteem, and for my career, at that time.

When have you been seen as experienced and felt that you had to know it all? Are you looking at not only yourself, but the environment you're operating in? How can you contextualise it and how can you ask for support? That is how you will gain more trust with others around you.

Trust and leaders placing their trust in you

As a leader, you need to place trust in those you lead.

This applies to you being the leader and placing your trust in someone else. Trusting them affects their Way of Being and their ability to make decisions, be vulnerable, ask questions, and lead others as they trust in themselves. They can do this because, in part, they're trusted by those whose authority matters – you. I am not saying you trust everyone – please use the appropriate 'Seven Assessments of Trust' that I shared with you in chapter one.

There are three clear examples of this in my career – two at a stage of being promoted to the next level, where the leaders trusted me and had my back, and one where I trusted the counsel of someone wiser who had also displayed total trust in the way that I led.

Prudy Gourguechon, who I mentioned in chapter one, wrote in the 2018 *Forbes* article 'Why Inspiring Trust and Trusting Others are Essential Leadership Capacities Within Bounds' that "the capacity for trust, both to trust others and to inspire trust is a fundamental character trait every leader with great responsibility must have."

As I shared with you previously, I joined the company my father worked for in 1988. While still at university, I was interviewed by Bruce Giles, the Managing Director of the Marks & Spencer food division, for the logistics arm of the company. He offered me a role as a management trainee when I graduated. For two years, he was my line manager. For six years, he was my sponsor in the organisation. He promoted me to my first senior management position as a site manager and helped my development immeasurably.

However, it all could have gone horribly wrong one evening in the bar of a hotel, where I heard him talking about leaders in his division and what a poor job some of them were doing. As a young management trainee, I went up to him and said, "You should tread carefully about how you speak about others so openly." He has since shared with me that he looked at me and thought, "This guy is either stupid or there's something about him." He chose to believe the latter, and as they say, the rest is history! I always felt he had my back and was supporting my career development, which went from strength to strength with his backing. This is the 'I' and 'S' in the Assessments of Trust – I felt that he was invested in me and was sincere in that. It was that company I left to join the company where I found myself leading (or not) the industrial dispute within a month of leaving, where I'd lost my sponsor.

In 2006, I joined National Foods in Melbourne, Australia, as the Group Executive of Logistics and Planning. I have already shared the story of leadership in safety there. In 2010, after the business was acquired by Lion Nathan, my remit on the executive team had grown exponentially. My boss Ashley Waugh, who was the CEO, backed me continuously and asked me to take more accountability for more functions of the business from 2006 to 2009. Without his trust in me and my ability to lead cross-functionally and deliver results, I would not have been asked to take on these additional areas of responsibility. It is in part because of his continued backing that I consistently led the delivery of these results.

In April 2006, I came out to Australia for my second interview with Ashley and to meet my future colleagues. At the same time, I had been asked to take on a new leadership role in Wincanton, the UK Logistics organisation that I was working for at the time, by the Group CEO, Graeme McFaull. The inner conflict about staying or going was considerable, both personally and professionally. I was trusted by Graeme and I trusted him, especially because of a very tricky client relationship that we jointly worked through together in my time there. It was because of this trust that I sought his counsel privately on this opportunity, believing that we could talk as humans and set aside our respective roles in the organisation. His counsel was for my best interests, not his. He basically gave me, in my head anyway, the green light to make the decision I wanted to and at the same time, not break his trust.

On the back of this conversation, and my two-day trip to Melbourne to meet Ashley and the National Foods leadership team, Paula, my wife, our two children, Sean (13) and Charlotte, (10) with our black Labrador, Lulu, moved to Australia in 2006. It is at this juncture I want to thank them for making their lives here, amid such upheaval from all that they knew and loved in the UK, as part of my definition of 'success' at that time. They have all done such an amazing job of making Australia home and I am profoundly grateful to them for this.

Those three stories are at the core of trust in leadership. As a leader, are you trusting those people who work for you? As a leader, do your leaders trust you? Do you know if your direct reports feel trusted? Ask these questions often.

As a footnote to these stories, on 14 February 2010, Paula and I hosted both Ashley and his wife Catherine, and Bruce and his wife Lita, at a dinner in our new home in Australia. Bruce and Lita were holidaying. For me, this was an incredible evening – having these two people who were (and still are) so important to me meeting one another and sharing stories was incredible.

It was also a way for me, and Paula, to thank them for their trust and counsel as well as to give back to two leaders in my life who had trusted me the most. I thank both Bruce and Ashley, as well as Graeme, publicly, for trusting me.

Maybe these examples don't resonate for you because you're always a listener, you're always curious, you're not inexperienced and you always place trust in others. Consider this – is that an assessment (belief) or an assertion (fact)? Can you 'ground it'?

If you feel the examples that I share don't resonate with you, can you find your own? What are your leadership stories of trust and what do your reflections tell you? You might want to write down your leadership stories of trust, both where you have been trusted by others and where you felt you didn't trust yourself.

Your stories of trust

Practical application

This section is about your stories of trust – an extension of the action you might have taken just now or taken earlier with your highlighter! Your stories will support you to be curious about trust in your life, what you see trust as being, and who you may or may not trust.

It's important for you to do this exercise before moving on. It tests your understanding of living in your stories and how they affect your view of trust, as well as understanding the distinction of assertions (facts) and assessments (beliefs).

Look at how I've reflected on my stories and chosen, at times, to re-narrate them, which opens me up to seeing trust in a different light.

Have a look at your life and your career. Break it down into a number of stories, then break each story down into assessments (beliefs) and assertions (facts). What new meaning has this made for you about these stories? Look specifically at stories of trust in your life – both personally and professionally – and think of the narratives that you've told yourself that have influenced these stories of trust, both positively and negatively.

It takes a conscious decision to reflect, and this isn't easy. You will need to make a choice to find the time and space to do this. You may need support from someone you trust to listen to you and help you work through them. When we get into some deep learning, we may need some other form of support in finding someone you trust to listen to you, and this could be confronting. You might need to work with a coach or even a doctor, a counsellor, or a psychologist to help you (I did).

Conclusion

You've learned where stories come from and about the Venn diagram of culture, family, and lived experience.

You've also learned about the distinction between assessments (beliefs) and assertions (facts), especially relating to your own stories and mine.

You've learned more about me and how to start relating your stories using assessments (beliefs) and assertions (facts) to your stories of trust.

The overriding barrier may be to overcome facing into your own stories and how they have shaped and are shaping your life, your leadership journey, your leadership actions, and behaviours as well as how you view trust.

By choosing to reflect on them, writing them down and learning from them, you'll start to see what you've thought is so, might not be so. It's important to complete all the exercises in this chapter before moving on to the next.

What's coming up?

We're going to move into my model and the New Ordering of Trust.

This model is based on my life experiences – both personal and professional. It combines my learning as an Executive Coach, and my leadership journey, to enlighten you in the deepest meaning of what trust is and how you can order it to support you as a human and as a leader.

Three

Trust begins and ends with self

My model of trust creates a New Order of what the components of trust are.

I outline them in full here, so that you can understand it before I break it down in detail, chapter by chapter, and then build on your capabilities in each part of the model. I call it a New Order because, as humans, we need order to make sense of things and live our lives harmoniously. The opposite is chaos. My New Ordering of Trust is creating a pattern of how you can make meaning of and create a feeling of what trust is from the inside out.

When you trust yourself, you will be in flow with yourself. Your relationships will be stronger, you will communicate more effectively, you will invest yourself in others' concerns sincerely, be vulnerable and be vulnerable to the actions of others, and consistently deliver on your commitments. You will hold others and yourself with legitimacy, and you will both trust and be trusted by others. Your brand will be enhanced, and you will link trust to the collective notions of team, society, and universal energy. By not seeing the pervasiveness of trust in all that you do, there is a risk that you will not hold others with as much legitimacy as they deserve, and your ability to deliver on your commitments will be diminished.

In the *Harvard Business Review* in 2020, Frances X. Frei and Anne Morriss wrote an article called 'Begin with Trust'. They present a model of trust called the Trust Triangle. I am not going into their model but want to share with you the part of their article that I believe delivers weight to my model, a New Ordering of Trust. They say, "The path to empowerment leadership doesn't begin when other people start to trust you. It begins when you start to trust yourself." I couldn't agree more.

You've also read stories of when I have both trusted myself and been trusted by others, as well as times where the opposite was true. I've asked you to take action by writing out your stories or at least taking time to reflect on them, to give evidence to these points above. The benefit of this chapter is so you can see the whole model in one, before I break it down for you in the next four chapters.

I'll outline the model and a New Ordering of Trust. I'll share how to trust your Way of Being, trust your Way of Doing and be in flow. How you can trust others and how you legitimise the other person. The notion of collective trust, and finally back to learning to trust yourself. Everything in this chapter will be covered in more detail in the next four chapters.

'Trust begins and ends with self' model and New Ordering of Trust

The whole model moves you from your Way of Being, to your Way of Doing, to trusting others, to the outer circles of collective trust. It's important to understand the whole model, a New

Ordering of Trust, so you can then work through each of the next chapters both to learn and apply the thinking. The concentric circles in the model lead back to the self.

CO'M model and New Ordering of Trust

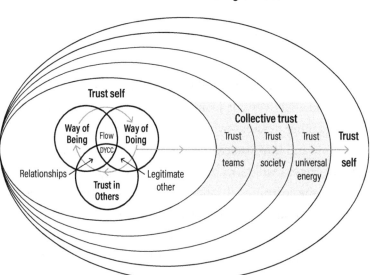

The model starts in the inner circle 'Trust self'. Stage one is understanding your Way of Being, which I will explain later. There is a distinction in life between our being – which is internal – and our doing – which is external. Our Way of Doing comes from our Way of Being, however it is our Way of Doing that others will observe most of the time. We are 'doing beings', both in action and in language. I will share with you how we take action through language, as well as the actions that we take which are observable to others.

Our Way of Doing is stage two in the model. When we understand both our Way of Being and our Way of Doing, we can be in flow. We unconsciously take action from a place that doesn't feel hard or take too much effort. For those who understand cricket, think of the cricketer who 'knocks off a hundred' before lunch and doesn't quite know how that person did it. For those who don't know cricket, think of the dancer who is on stage and comes off after the show feeling like it was effortless and the dancer floated on air. This is being in flow between your being and doing.

Stage three of the model is Trust in Others – both their Way of Being and their Way of Doing. Core to this is how you legitimise the other person – where they are coming from, what their stories are and how you can take care of their concerns with your actions. Here, I will talk about 'others' as one person in order to simplify the learnings. I talk about a larger number of people later in the model and book, by referring to it as 'collective trust'. An outcome of trusting others is stronger relationships with the other person whom you trust, as you both have each other's concerns at your heart and you're operating from a place of concern for them – which will take care of your concerns too.

At the heart of the Venn diagram in the inner circle of Trust self is 'DYCC' – as you have probably worked out this is 'delivering on your commitments, consistently'!

Stage four of the model is 'collective trust' – a combination of trusting your team, trusting society, and trusting a universal energy.

Stage five is bringing it right back to you – trusting self.

In a nutshell, that is my model and a New Ordering of Trust.

I've taken you through the whole model very quickly, so I would ask you to be curious and read on.

Stage one - Trust your Way of Being

Trusting your Way of Being is core to everything you do. It provides a new framework for sense-making and meaning-making. It helps you see new possibilities, invest yourself in others' concerns sincerely and work at a deeper level than simply your thinking through your brain.

CO'M model and New Ordering of Trust

As I shared in chapter one, your Way of Being comprises three aspects, according to ontological thinkers on this topic from the 1980s onwards. The three aspects are:

- Your language: how you use language to be clear in your communication, how you make meaning in language, both to yourself and to others, and how you coordinate action through language.

- Your moods and emotions: what you feel, the energy that is within you and how it drives you to take certain actions.

- Your physiology: what you sense and notice your body is telling you, which gives you a greater insight into how you see the world.

- The centre of the 'Way of Being' Venn diagram is trusting Self.

In my amended model (below) of the core ontological model of 'way of being' (above), I see our 'way of being' as being solely internal to us, and as such the domain of language is 'the language in your inner listening' or 'the stories that you tell yourself'.

'Way of Being' - this is internal to us

Adapted from Alan Sieler *Coaching to the Human Soul volume one*

Amanda Blake, founder of Embright.org, a website that "exists to explore and celebrate the wisdom of the human body", and author of *Your Body is your Brain*, presents it slightly differently by focusing on the 'embodied perception', the 'conceptual perception' and the 'emotional perception'. The words in brackets on her diagram is my interpretation of this using the ontological framework of our Way of Being:

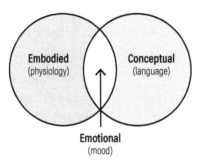

Adapted from Blake, A. (2019). *Whole Body-Mind Coaching in Coaches Rising: Neuroscience of Change*. Truckee, CA: Embright, LLC. With permission.

I share this alternative way of looking at your 'Way of Being' to expand on the Ontological view, and to show that it is becoming more 'mainstream' in its presentation to readers and learners today.

By seeing life through these lenses, it makes you more self-aware as a person and as a leader. It gives you an understanding of what you are thinking and how you communicate, how you feel, and what your body is telling you. It reveals how you see the world – if you can observe yourself in all three domains.

You might ask, "What has this got to do with trust? Why do I need to understand my language, my moods and my physiology to think about trust?" Trust is complex. Let's explore further.

Ask yourself – what are you observing right now in any one of the three domains that I've outlined to you? Are you hearing yourself tell a story about what you're reading? Are you feeling anything? What's the emotion or the energy that you're sensing and noticing in your body? By noticing any of these, they are your Way of Being in the present.

You may need to take some time and space to answer these questions. I've got to say, it's not easy observing oneself. You can observe yourself at any time and any place. Observe yourself in these three domains, starting with language. What am I thinking right now? In my moods and emotions, what am I feeling? What's the energy in my body? In my physiology, what am I sensing? What am I noticing? You can ask yourself any of these questions anytime of the day and in any place. That's what I call observing self.

Stage two – Trust your Way of Doing

Your 'way of doing' is observable by others and it is ultimately the domain of taking action.

'Way of Doing' – this is external to us and observable by others

"Language is action" – think about this. How can you take action without using language? You can't. In this context language includes not only what you say audibly, but what you write. It is observable by others, and they will judge/assess you by it.

Your behaviour is an action – it is the manifestation of how you take action, and your body language that others observe.

Ultimately the action you take is an action – that's pretty obvious. There is both a 'what action you take' and 'how you take it' that also relates to your behaviour others observe.

I'm going to introduce to you the notion of the question "for the sake of what?" and how we can be in flow, which is the intersection in the model between being and doing.

Without making the distinction of your Way of Doing, you will not be able to separate it from your Way of Being. It's important to be conscious of why you are doing what you are doing and what choices you are making. This will include how you take action in language, and it is your Way of Doing that others will see, feel, hear, and experience. That will relate directly to your brand.

CO'M model and New Ordering of Trust

Your Way of Doing is ultimately being effective in how you coordinate action and 'make meaning' for others through the effective use of audible language, the actions that you take and how you consistently deliver on your commitments. It is causally related to your brand.

Let me share with you an assessment (belief) of two world leaders to help you come to your own conclusion about this notion of Way of Doing, comparing Donald Trump (the outgoing President of the United States at the time of writing) and Nelson Mandela (former President of South Africa).

Trump is all about self and protecting his ego. In my assessment he is an ineffective communicator – he can't deliver a concise message consistently. He breaks commitments – repeal Obamacare, Mexico will pay for the wall. According to the *Washington Post*, he has broken 43% of the 60 key promises he has made. In my assessment his brand is selfish and for self. However, I acknowledge that after the 2020 Presidential election there are approximately 70 million Americans who disagree with me.

Mandela is about others and his legacy is associated with a nation reborn. His communication was concise and meaningful. He kept his commitments – he delivered the first fully democratic elections in South African history, and he did not stand for re-election after one term. His brand is selfless and for others – he wore the number six Springbok jersey at the 1995 Rugby World Cup final, which was previously the symbol of white supremacy in his country. He embraced that jersey to bring the nation together.

Both of these men have vastly different ways of being that led to vastly different ways of doing. It is their ways of doing that are being judged by others relative to their ego and legacy.

Core to knowing why you are doing what you are doing is being able to answer this one question – "For the sake of what?" I label this #forthesakeofwhat or #FTSOW, based on the work I do on LinkedIn, and how I use it in my Coaching Practice. It is the ultimate self-accountability question. From an extra doughnut, to 'taking on' the boss, to breaking a commitment, ask yourself – #forthesakeofwhat, every time.

When you are unconsciously competent, you leverage your experience and intuitively know what you are doing. The surgeon who completes a transplant, the sailor who trims the sail to that point where the boat is sailing in perfect harmony with the elements, the Grand Prix driver who finds him or herself in the fabled 'zone', or the CEO who has a day where everything goes to plan and something feels different, but you just don't know why. Doing comes from being, and what you're doing is how people trust you, because it is in your doing that you either do or do not consistently deliver on your commitments – which is the ultimate distinction of being trusted or not.

You might have a different view of Trump and Mandela, and I acknowledge that that may well be the case. However, ask yourself, "Are you making an assessment (belief) of trust around their doing?" If it is based around that – whatever your assessment (belief) is – that grounds my argument. I also ask you to consider who these two people were invested in – themselves or others' concerns? That is their way of being coming to the fore in the domain of trust.

You also might think, "I don't have the time to ask myself #forthesakeofwhat before I do something". You do. However, let's say you feel like you don't, then ask yourself straight after you have done something, and relate what you've done to that question.

You might say, "Well, one's brand is more than trust". Yes, it is. It's your message, image, tone of voice, language used (which is core to trust), the company one keeps, the activities one takes part in. However, trust and consistently delivering on your commitments are central to all of those.

Ask yourself, "What is my Way of Doing? How do people observe my Way of Doing and does that lead to them trusting me?" It could be about something like whether I'm fast or slow at a task. It's the behaviour that I demonstrate. How do others observe the way that I communicate? How do others observe whether I consistently keep my commitments or not? And do I know why I do what I do? This comes back to this #forthesakeofwhat question.

You could be self-conscious about asking others, "How do you see me?" If that is the case, then ask somebody who you feel you trust.

Stage three – Trust in Others

Trust in Others is about effective communication between you and the other person and you both consistently delivering on your commitments. This idea, this notion of 'the legitimate other', is the intersection between your Way of Doing and Trust in Others – all you need to remember here is that being invested in another, and their concerns, is central to 'the legitimate other'. I'll explain what I mean by 'the legitimate other' in chapter five.

CO'M model and New Ordering of Trust

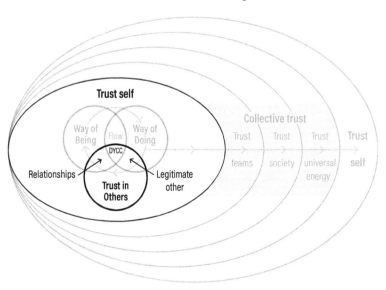

Building relationships is the intersection between trusting others and your Way of Being.

Without trusting others, your life will not be fulfilling, your relationships will not be as strong as they could be, and you will not be trusted by others.

Think about the importance of language and trusting others. How do you use language effectively to coordinate action and have purposeful conversations? Again, I will share more of this in chapter five.

Fundamental to building trust is to hold others as 'the legitimate other'. To trust someone else, you have to legitimise them as a human first and be invested in them as a human. You don't judge their story – their culture, their family, and their lived experience. Even if you don't agree with it, you legitimise their story as you legitimise your own. From that place, you can have a more meaningful conversation and/or relationship. This will support you to be a more effective leader of your diverse team – take a look, it is probably more diverse than you believe it to be when you overlay this lens.

Core to this notion of 'the legitimate other' is holding yourself as legitimate too. Too often, we allow our legitimacy to come from others and not from ourselves. If this is the case, then I suggest you observe your Way of Being to find your own inner legitimacy.

Helping others consistently deliver on their commitment to you is core to trusting others and being trusted by others. Building relationships is an outcome of legitimising the other and self, taking care of the other person's concerns, and communicating effectively. The inner circle (DYCC), consistently delivering on your commitments is the outcome.

You may have trusted someone and been hurt. In that context, using my framework or my model, look at what I shared with you in chapter one – the Seven Assessments of Trust, which is being <u>vulnerable</u> and being <u>vulnerable</u> to the actions of another, being <u>invested</u> in another's concerns and being <u>sincere</u> in that, as well as <u>reliability</u>, <u>competency</u>, and <u>capacity</u> – and doing all this <u>consistently</u>. When you were hurt, was the person invested in your concerns (I) and sincere in that (S), and/or open to being vulnerable (V) to your actions?

Ask yourself some questions:

- How well do I trust others?
- How well do I legitimise everyone that I come into contact with?

- How well do I hear their story?

- How strong are my relationships? If they're not as strong as you assess them to be, what part does trust have to play in that?

- The sum of trusting your Way of Being + trusting your Way of Doing + trusting others is the first part of trusting self – the first circle around this part of the model. The heart of this Venn diagram, the intersection of these three areas, is you delivering on your commitments.

Stage Four – Collective trust

Collective trust is the outer three circles – trust in your team (which as a CEO, is also your whole organisation), trust in your society, and trust in universal energy.

Trusting your team (and organisation, as the CEO) to deliver is what underpins delivering results, as well as having them trust you as a person and as a leader. Trusting the society you are a part of, and a leader in, is core to your legacy and the difference that you want to make in that society. Trusting universal energy gives perspective, meaning and context in your life. Bringing it all back to self, that grounds you and gives you an element of control.

CO'M model and New Ordering of Trust

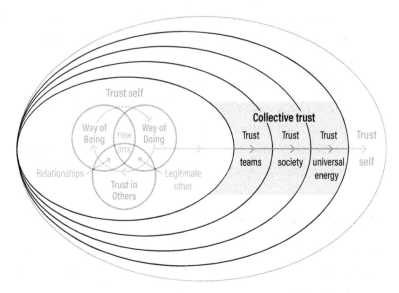

There is more to trusting another. As a leader, you operate in a wider domain. This needs to be built on by you trusting your team/organisation and your team/organisation trusting you. By doing this, both you and your team/organisation will deliver the results required by your customers and shareholders. However, if one or more of your team members is lacking in an element of the Seven Assessments of Trust, then you must look to yourself to either coach or 'performance up' the person in question through having the appropriate 'type of conversation'. See chapter five, for 'types of conversations'.

You are a leader in society by being a leader of and within your organisation. How you see and trust society has a direct relationship to your leadership role. You are not only a leader in your organisation, you are also a leader in society. Society is changing and leaders in business are more influential now than ever before in society. The fabric of the church, government and other traditional institutions, such as the formal media, are slower to adapt and lead in today's uncertainty and VUCA world. You have a role to lead both in your company and in society. Knowing how to trust society and having society trust you is fundamental to being a senior leader today.

How you are in touch with the universal energy of spirituality, or whatever you believe to be larger than life itself, is core to you trusting yourself. You need to trust in a universal energy that can guide you in some way. By being in touch with the universal energy, you will trust yourself as you rely on something that is bigger than all of what has gone before, to give you context and meaning to life.

I'm talking about religion if that's what you hear when you read this. I'm talking about spirituality if that's what you hear when you read this. I'm talking about something that is bigger than all of us, perhaps nature, if that works for you. For me, universal energy is anything that is bigger than what I've shared with you in terms of the team or society. It's whatever you make it.

Reflect on the trust in your team and how you see society and your role in it – both as a citizen and as a leader. Ask yourself, "Is there something bigger than all of this?" I call it universal energy. What do you call it? Do you ever bring it back to yourself and take control for yourself?

Stage Five - Trusting self

Finally, part five of the model, ends right back with you trusting self.

CO'M model and New Ordering of Trust

I realise that there's a lot to take in. You might want to go back and break it down into each section and look at the diagram at the beginning of the chapter. Or alternatively, keep reading, because I'm going to break each of these down now in the following chapters.

Conclusion

You've learned about the overview of my model of trust and how it's ordered:

- the three inner circles in trusting self – Way of Being, Way of Doing, Trust in Others
- the three intersections in the model – Flow, 'Legitimate other' and Relationships

- the centre of the inner circles – consistently delivering on your commitments
- the three outer circles – Collective trust
- the final outer circle – Trust self.

What's coming up?

The next four chapters will bring a breakdown of the whole model and New Ordering of Trust, with stories and frameworks that you can use in both your professional and personal life to help you build trust in yourself and others in you.

Your Way of Being is the start of the journey of trust. Unless you trust your Way of Being, you will not trust your Way of Doing, trust others or create collective trust. If you can trust your Way of Being, you will live a more fulfilled life. If you don't address your Way of Being and observe yourself from the inside out, then you will only live a Way of Doing which is not grounded or integrated with self.

I wake up every day and set out to live my purpose – to be a beacon for others. Unless I'm aware of (or observe) my Way of Being, I know I won't be my best self and deliver on my purpose. I will get into doing and not be aware of self. Being aware of self comes down to three things: What am I saying to myself? What mood or emotion am I feeling? What is my body telling me?

Why these three things? In language our self-talk creates our stories – whether I am feeling good or bad, energised or not, open to possibilities or not. Is my inner dialogue empowering me or disempowering me? If I don't listen to that voice, then I won't know what I'm thinking or feeling. I will just do. This is the language part of our way of being – our inner dialogue, which is not audible to others.

My feelings are the energy that I feel in me and they are also a manifestation of the mood that I am in. Alan Sieler quotes in his book *Coaching to the Human Soul volume two*, that our moods "are recurrent predispositions for action" – the mood we are in will predetermine the action that we take and the possibilities that we see.

My body tells me things. If I notice what it is telling me and acknowledge it, I can make meaning of it and that will help my feelings, my use of language and my actions – both to self and to others. This leads into this chapter and your Way of Being.

I will share with you all about Language, Moods and Physiology as we break open the first circle in the model.

Trust and language

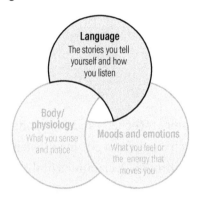

"Humans are meaning making machines."
— Alan Sieler, *Coaching to the Human Soul volume one.*

We make meaning through language – both in our inner listening (language in our being) and what we say audibly (language in our doing). I'd like to introduce you to what I mean by this through Fernando Flores' six aspects of language, their purpose in building trust and this idea of 'types of conversations'. Every conversation we have is a type of conversation, and in some way their purpose is related to trust.

Understanding how we make meaning, and how we coordinate action through the use of language, underpins how we understand trust, how we trust others and self, as well as how we deliver on our commitments and build relationships. You can't do any of this without language. How you think about the type of conversation you are going to have, and what you want to achieve from that conversation, is what builds trust.

In the model, there are six aspects of language as presented in Conversationsforaction.com that break down Flores' work:

1. Assessments
2. Assertions
3. Declarations
4. Requests
5. Offers
6. Commitments.

We covered assessments (beliefs) and assertions (facts) in chapter two, much of which come from our inner listening (our being). I will be taking you through declarations in this chapter, as well as a quick recap of assessments and assertions. I will cover requests, offers and commitments in chapters five and six.

> "Declarations are statements with a force of some authority behind them, which immediately bring about a change in circumstance and the generation of a different reality."
> — Alan Sieler, *Coaching to the Human Soul volume one.*

We can make 'private' declarations (in our inner listening – our way of being) and 'public' for others to hear (in our way of doing). The essence of their construct is the same in both domains of being and doing – hence it could be in either chapter regarding Being or Doing. I have chosen this one.

If you make a declaration that does not have the force Sieler refers to, or that does not generate a different reality, then it is either not a declaration or it is not a powerful one. This does not mean the declaration brings about a change in circumstance at the time, however it does mean that it must create a new reality in the mind of the listener (that can be you too!). A declaration is an incredibly powerful aspect of language and should be used sparingly. "Make America great again," and "Get Brexit done," were two immensely powerful declarations, both of which had authority behind them based on the people who said them. They also clearly created a new picture in the minds of listeners.

As the CEO, you will say to the board, in the domain of doing, "I will drive up EBITDA by 10%", "I will win that piece of business this financial year", "I will offer that role to that person by next week." You don't say, "I hope to drive EBITDA up by 10%", "I think we'll win that piece of business this financial year", "I will try to offer that role to the person by next week." None of these have authority or create a new picture in the mind of the listener. If you're really not sure, then don't make a declaration. Talk about it as being an opportunity or a possibility instead.

Understanding the importance of an audible declaration is core to how you make and deliver on your commitments so that people trust you.

Please note that there is a difference between a *declaration* and an *intention*. An intention is just shy of a declaration; it is more in the domain of a strong possibility. My advice is don't make a declaration unless you are going to commit to delivering it. If you are not sure, then share the idea as a possibility or an intention before you declare it audibly.

My private declaration (in my way of being), back in April 2020, was that I will write a book and I will have it published by Christmas in the same year. The fact that this book was published in 2020 means that I delivered on the commitment I made to myself in that declaration. When I shared that audibly with a small group of individuals, it created a new picture of me and my work in their minds. Conor – an author. What a scary picture to have created. My apologies to those who I created that new image for at the time!

Another public declaration in a 'way of doing' that I want to share with you was one my brother made at the beginning of the British summer in 2014. He is a headmaster, and tragically a pupil at his school died of a malignant brain tumour on 29 December 2013. Here is what my brother wrote on his 'Just Giving' page in 2014 – "The song 'I Will Walk 500 Miles' by The Proclaimers was one of Silas' favourites and so I have decided to run 500 miles this summer to raise money for The Brain Tumour Charity. This equates to 5.43 miles every day for 92 days (June 1st – August 31st)." I can say that he achieved his declaration and raised £4,129 for the Brain Tumour Charity, which was 206% of his goal. *(JustGiving. com)* Now that is both delivering on your commitments and your declaration! I am proud to be Simon's brother.

If you don't make good on your audible declarations, or you use them like confetti, eventually the trust in your vision will be eroded. You may be thinking that a declaration is an instruction, a way of getting people to do things. No, it isn't. You ask people to do things via a request or via an instruction. A declaration is envisaging something for them and you, and it creates the opportunity for them to follow you by acting on the declaration.

In summary, a declaration is a commitment that you make to yourself, which can either be made in your inner listening – a private declaration that nobody hears (being) or as a public audible declaration (doing), that others hear or read about.

Not all declarations are delivered. Is America great again? You can answer that yourself. Did you deliver on the EBITDA or bring on board that new customer? What if a declaration's not delivered, will trust automatically be broken or eroded? It depends on how you have communicated your progress towards that declaration to those who you created a new future for in what you said. Later, we will look at stage three of the commitment cycle – where it is your responsibility to communicate progress, even if the progress is not what you declared or committed it would be. If you don't communicate progress that the declaration will not be delivered, you will lose trust when the milestone date comes along. You may still lose trust by not delivering on your declaration, however the effective communication 'on the miss' will potentially build even greater trust through transparency, vulnerability, and authenticity.

I will cover the last three aspects of language – requests, offers and commitments – in chapters five and six, as these are aspects of doing in language. You will learn about a model in language called the commitment cycle. I will also cover types of conversations in the same, as these are aspects of doing in language. However, as a short introduction, think about every conversation you have as a type of conversation with a purpose and a KPI (objective) at the end of it. We'll talk more about this in those chapters.

Surely there's more than six aspects of language? Well there could be. However, see if what you think is an aspect of language is not already covered by these. If that's the case, then there may be, but I haven't found it so in the work that I do.

Looking at assessments (beliefs) and assertions (facts) that we covered in chapter two and declarations above, let's recap them here before we move on. Let's look at someone's name. Is that an assessment or an assertion? Is a name a fact? Yes, because the society that the person lives in deems a name on a birth certificate to be a fact. Think of the distinction of what society accepts as being true as being an assertion (fact). I do accept that in this current time of writing with the overused words 'fake news' and journalists trying to do their best with fact checking, this distinction is becoming increasingly blurred. Remember, a declaration paints a new picture of the future in the mind of the listener – which can be you too!

Practical application

What assessments are you making as a leader that you are presenting to your team as assertions? What declarations to yourself or audibly for others have you made recently? Were they really declarations or poorly worded assessments that you thought were declarations? For example, you may have said, "We must improve our wastage percentage by 10%." That is an assessment (belief). A declaration would be, "We will reduce our wastage percentage by 10% this financial year." Was it clear and unambiguous? Was it said with authority, and did you paint the picture of a new future for the listener (which might have only been you)?

For some it is exceedingly difficult to make a declaration as they feel it may unduly affect another. If this is you, perhaps you can make it a two-stage approach – firstly say, "I want to do X" (an intention), and then check how others feel about that. Then, as the second stage, declare "I will do X".

You might believe that you've made a declaration without meaning to, or not made an effective declaration when you meant to. You are making an assessment as you read this. A way to find out if your assessment of your declaration is grounded in reality is to ask those who heard it or read it. They are the ones who you wanted to create a new vision of the future when you made it. Think of something you want to do in the future. Can you make a declaration of it? If not, why not? Are you unsure of your ability to deliver? Is it possible and will others actually see the picture you want to paint for them?

Trust and moods

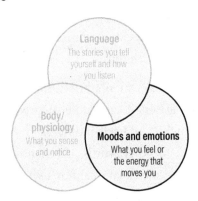

Moods are the essence of what you feel, not what you think. So often this distinction is missed when we are asked "how we are feeling", or you ask yourself, "how am I feeling?" Mastering this element of your way of being will change your life, as it will give you a new lens from which you make meaning of yourself, how you see others, the actions you see as possible and the world you live in.

Your moods provide you with a lens through which you make assessments, see possibilities, and take action. Moods are also predispositions for action.

I say to my clients, "Your mood predetermines your action", and ask them to make an assessment of that statement in their life. I have yet to hear a person disagree with this statement.

In my model of Trust, your mood predetermines your Way of Doing. I'll provide you with a distinction between moods and emotions, and I will also share the moods framework with you later in the chapter.

If feeling your emotions and your mood predisposes your Way of Doing, then observing it in your Way of Being will enlighten you to your actions and what is possible. You are the one who chooses what you give your energy to. Ultimately, you will make meaning of your mood in language as it comes down to an assessment (belief) of what you are feeling.

Robert C. Solomon says in his book *The Passions*, "once self consciousness has arisen, it cannot be suppressed ... One might continue to be cruel ... and self-indulgent ... but that person is now so by choice". In other words, if you now start to observe your moods and emotions you cannot switch that observation off – "it cannot be suppressed". I urge you to not suppress your newfound emotional self-awareness once it has arisen – that will not serve you well.

The distinction between moods and emotions that I'd like to share with you is that moods are longer lasting, and emotions are short-lived.

In *The Passions*, Solomon also shares that moods "are generalized emotions: an emotion focuses its attention on more-or-less particular objects and situations, whereas a mood enlarges its grasp to attend to the world as a whole without focusing on any particular object or situation."

In *The Field Guide to Emotions*, Newby and Watkins, experts in the field of emotions and emotional literacy, say that our emotions "are energy that puts you in motion". I make a statement to my clients, "An emotion is your energy in motion." Newby goes on to say in *The School of Emotions* via webinars "that every human has emotions and that we are emotional beings. Emotions are neutral. They're not positive or negative. They are either serving us or not serving us in the moment. Emotions are a source of information and every emotion has a purpose. An emotion is a domain of learning and it's as important as our intellect. Emotions cannot be separated from reason, and they're not random and unpredictable. We can learn to trust our emotions." In the book *The Field Guide to Emotions*, Newby and Watkins outline more than 200 distinct emotions that we can learn from.

For Alan Sieler in *Coaching to the Human Soul volume two*, emotions are "shifts in predispositions for action" and moods are "recurrent predispositions for action".

Susan David – psychologist, speaker and author of the bestselling book *Emotional Agility* – shared on a podcast with Brené Brown (Research Professor at University of Houston) that "we are never not in an emotion". Just think about that as you read on. I feel, and believe, that by using the double negative here it accentuates the statement.

As Ashkan Tashvir summarises in his book *Human Being*, "Moods impact every one of us more than we may realise throughout our entire lives. The decisions you make and the actions you take directly reflect the health of your relationship with your moods."

Having shared with you the importance of moods in your life and made the important distinction between a mood and an emotion, now I'd like to share with you the moods framework in an experiential way.

Practical application

On a piece of paper, draw a horizontal line that is below mid-way on the piece of paper. I'm going to talk to you about moods that are 'above and below the line'. Now draw two vertical lines so that you've got a six-box model with three boxes above the line and three boxes below the line. Hopefully, there is more room in the top three boxes than the ones below.

Label the top left box as 'peace', the top middle as 'ambition' and the top right as 'curiosity'. Then label the bottom left box as 'resentment', the middle bottom as 'resignation' and bottom right as 'anxiety'. The moods in this diagram are not the only moods in life, however these arguably are the six core moods in life.

Those are the six core moods in the moods framework – three above the line and three below the line. The top is the opposite or the antithesis of the bottom. Above the line, we are in a meta mood of acceptance, feeling empowered and open to learning – "in a growth mindset," as Carol Dweck might say. Below the line, we are in opposition to something. We are disempowered, closed to learning or, as Carol Dweck might say, in "a fixed mindset". If you were to draw an arrow pointing horizontally, all of those three moods above the line could be described as in acceptance, empowered or growth. Below the line, those three moods are in opposition to, disempowered or fixed. I prefer to use the word 'mood' instead of 'mindset', because it relates to our energy and our feelings.

Draw arrows pointing down above the words 'peace', 'ambition' and 'curiosity' (hence leaving more space at the top of the model). Instead of looking at this model from a horizontal perspective, we're now looking from the vertical perspective. Above the arrow above 'peace', write the words 'it is so'. Above the arrow above 'ambition', write the word 'possibilities'. Above the arrow above 'curiosity', write 'uncertainty', 'not knowing' and VUCA.

In this moods framework, if we're looking vertically, what does 'it is so' mean? The word 'It' refers to whatever you are in acceptance of, or in opposition to. It could be a relationship breakdown that you might be either at peace with, or resentful of. It might be your role that has been made redundant. It might be a bereavement where a loved person or animal has passed. It is whatever is placing you in a mood of potential resentment towards it. It is you being in opposition to it and you feel disempowered. Conversely, if you are at peace with it, you are in acceptance of it, more empowered and would be open to learning.

The word 'possibilities' above ambition is about being open to possibilities. It's another way of framing ambition and resignation. Think of yourself in a mood of resignation, where you might say, "I can't be bothered. It's not worth it. I've seen it all before." Are you open to possibilities? I doubt it, especially as the mood of resignation has an element of passive disempowerment to it. However, if you are in a mood of ambition, you are ambitious about seeing, feeling, and working towards possibilities. That might be the ambition of being the next CEO, being the next chair of the board. It may be the ambition of the possibility of a new relationship, a conversation you are going to have (or want to have), or a milestone that you are going to hit. It's ambition in seeing possibilities, being open to them and then taking action from that mood towards the possibility you envision.

In relation to the words 'uncertainty' and 'not knowing' that you have written above 'curiosity' on your model, I asked you to write down VUCA too – volatile, uncertain, complex, and ambiguous – a phrase used in business leadership language today as shared with you in chapter two. We live in an uncertain world, a VUCA world. If you are in a mood of curiosity, you are open to the uncertainty of the time as well as being okay with 'not knowing'. There is a key difference between uncertainty and not knowing – uncertainty is a constant and is something we have to learn to live with and 'deal with' every day. If you are in a mood of anxiety, you are in opposition to or closed to the uncertainty, which will not predispose you to 'walk towards or embrace the uncertainty'. If you are curious and choose to shift your mood above the line to curiosity (if you were below the line in a mood of anxiety), you will be more open to the uncertainty and, as a leader better able to lead in the VUCA world, by being curious, open to possibilities and being a conscious listener. However, not knowing is different. There will always be times when you don't know something, and it too leaves you with a choice, however it is a different choice, it is a choice to learn. A way of taking action with not knowing is to ask questions or make a request of someone to learn and find out more about what it is that you don't know. An ontological coach colleague of mine, Deanne Duncombe, wrote in response to something I posted on LinkedIn on this subject: "An interpretation that I like for 'not knowing' is that it is an assessment that I don't YET have the ability to take action in a given situation. This enables me to accept that 'not knowing' is ok – I can learn to take action (come to 'know') if I choose." *(My LinkedIn Post October 2020 on uncertainty and not knowing.)*

Now take the word 'ambition' and write two words below it – 'shallow' and 'deep'. In this framework, we need to be in both a deep and shallow mood of ambition to stay there. We need both to stay above the line. What do I mean by 'shallow'? In shallow ambition, we have passion and enthusiasm. We need passion and enthusiasm to be in a mood of ambition to see the possibilities, however that in itself is not enough. Shallow ambition is passionate enthusiasm – "Yeah, come on. Let's get on the rooftop. Come on, gang!"

We have to have deep ambition, as well as shallow, to remain in a mood of ambition. Deep ambition is courage, patience, and perseverance. You could put the word resilience there as well if you like. However, using the distinction Ashkan Tashvir uses in his book *Human Being*, 'resilience is "elasticity" … a quality that enables you to bounce back to your original form, or even stronger, when life knocks you down." It is different from perseverance in my context; however, courage, patience, and perseverance are all a part of being resilient and bouncing back.

Now circle the word 'acceptance', which hopefully is to the left of Peace on your model. You might be saying to yourself, "Getting to an overall mood of peace and acceptance, that's quite a tough thing to do," and I would agree with you. Jim Dethmer from *The Conscious Leadership Group* talks about the "four A's of acceptance" and this is a process we can go through to find true peace.

- The first A is 'acknowledge', and it is relative to the 'it is so', specifically to the 'it'. Simply acknowledge. It's not simple to do, but simply acknowledge that 'it' has happened. You don't have to accept it yet. It's like an outside-in.

- The second A is 'allow', which is an inside-out. You're allowing it to come into you, physiologically. You feel it. You may still be fighting it, but you feel it.

- The third A is 'acceptance'. I know and you know that we can still feel something. We can accept but we're kind of still fighting it. We've cognitively accepted it, but have we fully accepted it?

- The fourth A is 'appreciation'. My sense making of the fourth A is that is where we find true peace. Once we have 'appreciation', we have true peace. I do acknowledge that with deep trauma it may not be possible to ever get to this fourth A.

You can now write '4 'A's of' above the word Acceptance to the left of Peace on your model.

I'm also not saying that moods below the line are bad and moods above the line are good. But if you live your life 24 hours a day, 365 days a year, below the line, that probably won't predispose you to effective actions. However, there are times when being in a mood of resentment, anxiety or resignation can be helpful to your Way of Being.

If there's a bereavement or a relationship breakup, feeling angry, which is an element of a mood of resentment, is no bad thing. We need to feel that anger and then work through it so that we can acknowledge, allow, accept and then in some way appreciate that person having been in our life.

Anxiety, being concerned and worried at times, is no bad thing. It makes us think. It gives us the opportunity to reflect and feel the uncertainty. However, if we live in a constant mood of anxiety, we will not be able to embrace the uncertainty within which we live.

So, our moods predispose our actions. However, can you choose to shift your mood? Yes, you can – feel it, observe it, and label it, think of the possibilities and choices you have and then take action to shift it above the line. This is at the core of my coaching framework Observe|Choose|Act.

Here is my illustration of the Moods Framework – how similar is yours, having drawn it as you read the last part of this chapter?

Moods Framework

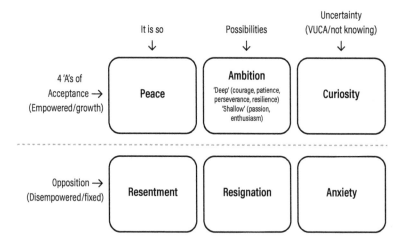

Adapted from Alan Sieler *Coaching to the Human Soul volume two*

You might think, "I can overcome my mood and not let it get in the way of what I'm going to do or achieve." You can find the energy to do that in the moment. However, unless you address and choose to shift your mood above the line, eventually you will be caught out by yourself and your mood. The moods above the line tend to be more energising and empowering moods than those below the line.

You may feel there is a potential incongruence between the mood you feel, if you are 'below the line', and how you need to present yourself to others in a particular situation – be it a leadership situation or a personal one. This may be so, or not. We will look at this in the next chapter, after I have further explained the distinction between 'Way of Being' and 'Way of Doing'.

How are you feeling right now? How are you labelling that feeling? Is it serving you well or less well? Do you feel above or below the line? Do you feel empowered or disempowered? Do you feel energised or not energised? Are you at peace with 'it is so'? As a client recently said to me when I shared this, "Can you ask yourself the question, 'is it so?'" which is actually leading to an assessment. Yes, you can!

I hope you can now see that your moods provide you a lens from which you make assessments, see possibilities, and take action. They are your predispositions for action. For Solomon, they "are the structures of our world" *(The Passions)*.

Trust and physiology

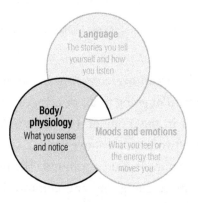

I have introduced to you earlier in the book the metaphor of 'taking the elevator from your mind to your body' and working on presencing in chapter three. What I am talking here is about far more than the generally accepted practice of mindfulness. As Ginny Whitelaw, the founder of the Institute for Zen Leadership put it in an interview with Joel Monk of Coaches Rising in January 2020 "Mindfulness doesn't stop at the neck". I love that – for me that statement embodies everything I am going to share with you about 'taking the elevator from your mind to your body'.

Not only do we 'live in our stories', which I shared with you in chapter two, but 'our stories live in us'. They are embodied. Another way of looking at my distinction of where our stories live is using the accepted psychological terms of 'explicit memory' (we live in our stories) and 'implicit memory' (our stories live in us). You are able to re-narrate the stories that you tell yourself by getting in touch with your physiology and rewiring your neural pathways.

There are cultural associations here too in how you observe your own body and also how you observe others. As your stories are made up of your culture, family and lived experiences, that has a direct influence on how you notice your physiology and how you make meaning of others' body language too. Be aware of this as you read this next part of the book and also as you observe others and make meaning of their body language – what is embodied in theirs that comes from their culture, family and lived experience, and what is embodied in yours? This is also a key part of holding a person as 'the legitimate other' (to come in chapter five).

It is not only the Ontological thinkers and writers, including myself, who have this belief. Amanda Blake, Founder of Embright.org and author of *Your Body is Your Brain*, writes in her book, "each one of us has embodied our own unique set of associations, which emerge out of the culture we live in, the activities we take on, and our early relationships. So it turns out it's not just your brain that's your social and emotional sense organ. *It's your entire body*".

Without noticing what's going on in your body, you will miss the most important signal of where trust really lies. I use the term 'noticing' (introduced to me in a Coaches Rising training session by Nicholas Janni, International Leadership Coach and founder of Peak Performance Presence and author or *Leader as Healer*) as I am asking you to 'notice', not to think or even feel what is going on in your body. Don't put a label to it or try to conceptualise it when you first sense it, simply sit, or rest, with it and 'notice'. This is where the magic lies.

In James Joyce's short story *A Painful Case*, "Mr Duffy lived at a little distance from his body." Think about that statement. How can you 'live a little distance from your body'? It is not possible – you and your body are one. It is not a 'thing' that is separate from you. It tells you things. What can you learn from it, and how can you use it to trust yourself and others? It will guide you and support you in making good on your commitments.

Your stories live not only in your brain, but in the whole of your broader nervous system. It is the nervous system where learning and change happens. Let's find more information about your stories from your senses and feelings. I call this 'taking the elevator from your mind to your body', which serves as a metaphor.

We are born and die with the same biological nervous system, save for some neurogenesis in early childhood. However, the nervous system is continually changing its structure, so it is continually a different nervous system in reality. It is this nervous system that enables you to see from the inside-out rather than the outside-in.

My interpretation of this continuous change is that over time your nervous system 'hardens' with your experiences. New connections between neurons occur and consolidate, and sometimes connections lessen as new ones develop. Here's a metaphor that I like to use: it's like an electrical system which once was loose and, over time, hardens and frays. By looking deeper inside yourself, you can find the stories that shape your thinking and how you see the world. Your stories live in you, in your electrical system. By 'taking the elevator from your mind to your body' you will find ways to trust your intuition – I did.

Mind to body elevator

Top floor
Cognition/thinking/language

Middle floor
Sense

Notice

Basement
Being grounded

Before I ask you to explore going deeper inside yourself, you may be asking what intuition is. There have been many studies in this space, from Jung in 1933 to Epstein in 2004, as referenced by Michael Pratt (Boston College Carroll School of Management) and Erik Dane (Rice Business School, Houston) in their paper 'Exploring Intuition and its Role in Managerial Decision Making'. In their paper they argue that there are "four characteristics that make up the core of the construct: intuition is a (1) non-conscious process – it occurs outside of conscious thought (2) involving holistic associations – environmental stimuli are matched with some deeply held (non-conscious) category, feature or pattern (3) that are produced rapidly, which (4) result in affectively charged judgments – that such judgements often involve emotions." My reading of this, and how it aligns with your Way of Being, is that intuition is clearly outside of the domain of the brain and lies in the wider nervous system, that it links with the stories that live in you, that it comes 'in the moment' and your assessments that come from your intuition are linked directly to the energy in you.

This notion of stories living 'in you' is important, because as you look to re-narrate your stories, you want to find the right ones – the ones that drive you. It's important to have a way of understanding yourself – a picture, if you like, to help you break the subject down. If you don't make these links to your body, you may not go deep enough to find the stories that are shaping how you see the world.

By being more in touch with my physiology, I became more grounded and as such I can go 'deeper' into the stories I'm telling myself and make a different meaning of them. And by having a metaphor or picture of how to understand myself and my Way of Being, it helps me make sense of what I think and feel.

Leading thinkers in this space are Alan Sieler in *Coaching to the Human Soul volume three*, Fernando Flores in *Understanding Computers and Ambition*, Humberto Maturana and Francisco Varela in *Autopoiesis and Cognition*, Dr Dan Siegel in *The Developing Mind*, Paul Zak in his January 2017 *Harvard Business*

Review article entitled 'The Neuroscience of Trust' and Amanda Blake in *Your Body is Your Brain*.

The basic link between our nervous system and our brain is important. By understanding this, it will help put into context how your stories live in you and how your physiology is central to your intuition and your Way of Being.

When I sit at my desk, taking the time to meditate and notice my breathing, I'm able to concentrate for longer and observe myself both as a learner and as a worker. When I notice that my feet are not grounded when I'm at my desk, I know I'm not concentrating as much as I'm capable of doing. By shifting my feet so they are grounded and fully touch the floor, I'm able to focus on my action – be it writing my book (I've just shifted my feet right now) or working with an executive in a coaching session. I'm able to listen more effectively as a coach and not live in my stories but listen to and feel the stories that I am being told by another.

Let's get further into the science and biology of this, because my New Ordering of Trust is based in science and biology, not only philosophy. The University of Queensland Brain Institute writes that "Neurons (also called neurones or nerve cells) are the fundamental units of the brain and nervous system, the cells responsible for receiving sensory input from the external world, for sending motor commands to our muscles, and for transforming and relaying the electrical signals at every step in between. More than that, their interactions define who we are as people."

"Neurons are information messages. They use electrical impulses and chemical signals to transmit information between areas of the brain and between the brain and the rest of the nervous system. Everything we think, feel, and do would be impossible without the work of neurons and their support cells" according to the National Institute of Neurological Disorders and Stroke.

Those two references are so important in understanding how fundamental the nervous system is to our Way of Being and how we think and feel from the inside out, due to these neurons.

Humberto Maturana and Francisco Varela began their book *Autopoiesis and Cognition* with the line, "Man knows and his capacity to know depends on his biological integrity; furthermore, he knows that he knows." Maturana and Varela are two of the early thinkers and biologists in this field of neurons. This unashamedly, for me, challenges Descartes' notion of "I think, therefore I am", written in his *Discourse on Method*, written in 1637.

Dr Dan Siegel, a clinical professor of psychiatry at the UCLA School of Medicine and the founding co-director of the Mindful Awareness Research Centre at UCLA, as well as being a Distinguished Fellow of the American Psychiatric Association, is at the forefront of bringing science to this subject of physiology, and to what I share with you as the third element of your Way of Being – your physiology. I was privileged to hear firsthand in a lecture with him in 2019 through Coaches Rising Transformative Presence Coach training where he shared some of his work. He stated that there are five physiological changes that change the structure and function of your brain by working within the body. In his book *The Developing Mind*, he shares that while working with 18 interns, he found that the integration in the brain with the body is the basis for "healthy regulation, regulating your mood, your emotions, your thoughts, your behaviour, your narrative capacity to cultivate meaning and your morality". Given his rigour and scientific-based evidence on how our physiology is so connected to our brain and how we see the world, I believe it gives more credence to the work of the early biologists, Maturana and Varela, who shaped Ontological thinking, and whose work is at the core of the concept of physiology being so central to your Way of Being.

As I said earlier, I see this as an electrical system with many wires in it, which I accept is not a purist view of the nervous system or neuroplasticity, which is more related to the neural pathways in the brain. However, I am trying to make meaning of it for you, without going too deep into the biology (which I may already have done?). When we're born, this electrical system is all floppy and we can do nothing but feel the electricity moving through it. We can't talk, share our feelings, or make meaning in language. Only as we grow into infants, toddlers, and then children who go off to school do we start to make meaning in language. At this point, I see our electrical wiring as starting to harden. This may be taking the biology too far, as what actually happens is new connections develop, not harden. However, the way I explain it is the nervous system hardens further as we grow through ado-lescence, young adulthood, and into adults. We can loosen it and reshape it by 'getting in touch with our neurons' or learn from them as they change. When that happens new neural connec-tions develop, which we can use to re-narrate our stories.

You can get in touch with your inner physiological self by med-itating or presencing and by 'taking the elevator from the mind to the body'. Part of what happens in this exercise is you are mimicking your body that is constantly sending information to the brain like, how you are feeling, how you are digesting your food, how you are experiencing the world outside of your body. The rate of information traveling from our gut to our brain in volume, through the Vagus nerve, is far greater than from our brain to our gut. According to Amanda Blake, as shared earlier, author of *Your Body is Your Brain*, in a Coaches Rising workshop in September 2020, "this transfer of information is 8–9 times greater from gut to brain than brain to gut". Given this, noticing what is going on physiologically below the neck is fundamental to being an observer of self and this observing is part of the equation of trusting self.

Later in the chapter, I'll share an exercise that you can do to 'take the elevator from the mind to the body and back' as though you are following the neurons.

This subject and its importance links directly to leadership and to business performance too. In his 2017 *Harvard Business Review* paper 'The Neuroscience of Trust', Paul Zak states that "neuroscience research shows that you can do this (create a culture of trust) through eight key management behaviours that stimulate the production of oxytocin, a brain chemical that facilitates teamwork". He also states that "compared to people at low trust companies, people at high trust companies report 74% less stress, 106% more energy at work, 50% higher productivity, 13% lower sick days, 76% more engagement, 29% more satisfaction with their lives and 40% less burnout". Make no mistake, this link between the brain and our nervous system is an important subject, not only for yourself but for your organisational culture too.

You may think if you know your biology, "where's the amygdala in all this?" In Leah Weiss's 2016 *HBR* article 'A Simple Way to Stay Grounded in Stressful Moments', she writes "The amygdala, located in the brain's medial temporal lobe, is the part of the brain that detects and processes fear". This response is important because, in times of extreme fear, it is important to notice the amygdala and get into fight or flight mode, rather than taking the time to presence oneself to the neurons and the nervous system. It actually does more than process fear, however fear is the emotion most associated with the amygdala. However, how often in a personal or professional context do you really experience this level of fear? It's not as if a rhino was running at you in the Maasai Mara in Kenya – which actually has happened to me when I was visiting with my brother Simon, and sister-in-law Katy, while they lived in Kenya. But that's a story for another day!

Practical application

So how do you 'take the elevator from your mind to your body', or even from your body to your mind? To start the process of getting in touch with those deeply held stories, sit, meditate, and notice your breathing first. Breathing is the gateway to the body. Count to five breaths in and seven breaths out. Picture an elevator which is stuck in your head – which is where most of us live in the cognitive domain. The elevator is on the top floor. It's in our head and the doors may be open or closed. Picture getting into the elevator. The doors are open. Mentally press 'B' for basement. Allow your breathing and mind to flow to your lower body – your heart, your hara region (your belly). If you can, existentially picture yourself getting out of the elevator when you are at 'B', and walking around inside you. What do you notice? What stories are lurking down there? Are they helping you or are they hindering you? How do you want to re-narrate them?

After 10 minutes of this deep breathing and inner exploration, get 'back in that elevator', mentally press the top floor button and return up into your mind. Now what meaning are you making of those stories? What changes do you want to make to them and your Way of Being, possibly to your mood or the energy flowing in you? This is a choice. Exit the elevator and put this into practice.

You might like to keep a notebook and write down what you were doing at a particular time, then answer these two questions relating to that time: How was my breathing? What did I notice going on in my body? Don't try to make meaning of it – simply notice and write down what you notice. It might be 'shoulders tight', 'shallow breathing', 'fiddly hands' or even 'feet tucked behind the leg of the chair'.

Have you ever really focused on your body, your breathing and what you notice physiologically when you are not focused, or when you are stressed? Have you ever noticed your physiology when you are telling yourself a self-limiting story? You can take action by first noticing your breathing and where you are breathing from. When you take the time to notice any physiological senses, note them down and relate them and a theme to the situation. After a week or a month, ask yourself, "What are the themes? What are the trends that I am sensing and noticing in my body at particular times?"

Why is it so important to focus on your physiology as much as your thinking in a cognitive domain? According to Weiss in her *HBR* 2016 article, "our bodies are the quickest, surest way back to the present moment when our minds are lost in rehashing the past or rehearsing the future." That says it all for me.

It is so important to 'be present' in life to be able to be in the moment and have clarity of thought. This comes from all aspects of your way of being – cognitive, emotions and physiology. Being present is central to trusting self.

Techniques I have for this (becoming 'present') are in three ways:

- I sense/notice my body – what is it telling me right now? It can only be now, that is all the body has.

- What energy am I feeling right now? Then I put a label to that energy, which in essence is labeling it as an emotion or mood.

- I ask myself this very simple question – "where are you now?". Literally where are you now. When my mind starts to wander to another place, this question takes me geographically to where I am right at that moment – it might be in bed, it might be in my office, it might be on a walk or on the golf course. I find it centres me to focus on the actual place I am right at that very second, which brings me to the present and 'out of' images/stories in my mind that may not be serving me well.

At a more 'basic' level, your wellbeing is inextricably linked to the third domain of your Way of Being – your physiology. Using the four pillars of health from Dr Rangan Chatterjee, in his book *Feel Better in 5*, consider this for your wellbeing linked to your physiology:

1. Relax – take time out every day.
2. Eat – make good choices.
3. Move – every day do some exercise and stretching.
4. Sleep – 7 to 9 hours in every 24 hours.

Barriers to this include not slowing down and making the choice to observe your physiology, not taking the time "to feel better in 5", and not asking for help. You can have it if you practise it. You've got to make it a routine and a habit in your daily life.

As Gary Player, the world famous South African golfer, is reputed to have said, "the harder I practice, the luckier I get". On research, it appears that, in 1962, Player attributes this saying to fellow golfer Jerry Barber. Regardless, I think it is a great maxim, and with regards to noticing your physiology – practise and you will get luckier!

Finally, I heard this anecdote somewhere when researching the relative importance of our heart to our brain but can't recall where. I ask you now to picture the heart talking to the brain as in a cartoon. The heart is saying, "Hey buddy, you work for me, not the other way around". I love that, it says it all, with no beating heart, there is no functioning brain!

Conclusion

You've learned all about your Way of Being and how it is in the three domains of language, moods, and physiology. You've learned about how your Way of Being is intrinsic to your Way of Doing.

What's coming up?

Your Way of Doing and how that relates to your Way of Being and being in flow.

Five

Trust your Way of Doing

CO'M model and Ordering of Trust

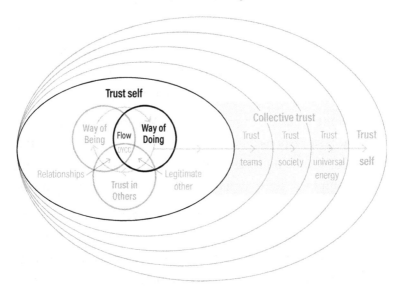

Once you're aware of your Way of Being, you can then choose your Way of Doing using my Observe|Choose|Act framework that I've mentioned in previous chapters. The question that we can all ask ourselves at any time is "For the sake of what?", or from a humanistic lens, "For the sake of whom?", which I'll refer to from now on as #FTSOW.

In this chapter, you'll learn how your audible language is a major part of your Way of Doing, particularly around how you talk about commitments with other people in order to consistently deliver on them and build trust. As evidence of this, I'll take you through a model called the 'commitment cycle' and share with you how you can categorise 'types of conversations' that you have in order to be purposeful with every conversation you have, which builds trust. Your actions and your Way of Doing create your brand – what you're seen as/known for – as a leader, and your brand is inextricably related to being trusted by others.

When you trust your Way of Being and your Way of Doing, you will be in flow – effortlessly bringing positive and empowering energy to your life, your relationships, and your leadership. I'll share more about this aspect of trust in this chapter.

If you don't focus on improving your Way of Doing and consciously take responsibility for it in the actions you take, the behaviour you demonstrate and the language that you use, your relationships will suffer, and trust will be less evident in your life.

Think of two extremes in the context of coaching, when a commitment has been made by me to support you working through a concern. If I'm not self-aware of my actions, my behaviour, and my language, I will not be trusted by you. Consider this approach by me (which I trust you will never experience) – me lounging in a chair and looking at my phone when you're sharing your story or your concern, then looking up and saying, "Sorry, what did you say?" Now consider me sitting in a posture where our energy and our flow are aligned, and there is a demonstration of conscious listening by my asking you questions in the domain of the concern that you are outlining, or the story that you're sharing. Which of these two characters are you likely to make a request of and trust working with as a coach? I'm sure I know which. I'm also sure you could swap this picture from a coach relationship to a leadership relationship with somebody who you've worked for. It is your Way of Doing and how you deliver on your commitments that is what others will assess as to whether they trust you or not.

I'll share with you the four aspects that make up your Way of Doing, and one that brings your Way of Being and your Way of Doing together. The four aspects are #FTSOW, the 'commitment cycle' and delivering on your commitments, 'types of conversations' and your brand, and the thing that brings your Way of Being and your Way of Doing together is you being in flow.

Trust and 'For the sake of what/whom?'

I introduced you to #FTSOW as the first stage of grounding your assessments in chapter two. However, it's much bigger than that. It is the ultimate self-accountability question that you can and should ask yourself all the time, in regard to your Way of Doing. You can and should ask yourself this question before you do or say anything (and saying is doing). It is an action in my life and coaching Observe|Choose|Act framework. If you don't do this before you do or say something, then do it afterwards to learn and reflect from your action in your Way of Doing.

This question links to your purpose. It provides accountability to yourself and ensures you take responsibility for what you do and say. It helps you think about the other person in your relationship and the conversation that you have with them, and it will causally link to how people trust you or not.

Let's start with Simon Sinek and his 'Why?' question. On 29 September 2009, during his TED talk, Sinek presented his 'golden circle' – why, how, and what. His model has three concentric circles with 'why' in the centre, followed by 'how', and 'what' around the outside. He shared that, "Very few people/organisations know why they do what they do." By 'why', he means their purpose, their cause, or what their belief is. His thesis is that the inspired leaders and organisations think from the inside out – they start with 'why'. "People don't buy what you do. They buy why you do it."

He builds on this with neuroscience and associates it with the neocortex brain, where the outside circle of what "corresponds with our analytical brain, which is where we make meaning and language. The middle two sections, why and how, come from our limbic brain, where this is made up of our feelings like trust and loyalty. It is also responsible for all human behaviour, all decision making, and it has no capacity for language." He asks us all to consider, "If you don't know why you do what you do, how will you get people to be loyal to you?"

Loyalty is part of trust, so *in this context* they are interchangeable. It is interesting that he regards trust and loyalty as feelings – which, in part, they are – as they have links to energy flows. However, they are so much more than that. It's about your purpose, your cause, your belief, which gives you reason to be who you are and do what you do.

He also 'grounds the assessment' that I made – a process which I shared with you in chapter four – of how your Way of Being and your physiology link directly with your Way of Doing. He does this by iterating that your limbic brain links to your feelings, moods, and emotions. The limbic brain is regarded as the emotional centre of the brain – so it is more than relating to feelings. This is living and leading from the inside out.

The question #FTSOW can have the notion of purpose in it and can be used for purpose, cause, and belief. I've shared my purpose of being a 'beacon for others' a few times now. I can ask myself, "#FTSOW – does what I'm about to say or do align with my purpose?" However, it goes the extra mile by asking others for the sake of what/whom **in the moment**, as well as at the deeper level of Sinek's why.

Practical application

Here's how it can work in practice. The answers to these questions will ensure you hold yourself accountable for what you do or say in the moment:

- For the sake of whom am I going to take this action?
- For the sake of what am I going to say what I'm about to say?
- For the sake of what am I going to make this post on social media?
- For the sake of what am I going to say this to my boss or a customer?
- For the sake of what am I going to do this thing, or be with this person?

- For the sake of what am I going to have this extra doughnut or glass of wine?
- For the sake of what am I going to exercise today?
- For the sake of whom am I going to shift my energy from working, say, 12-hour days, to focus on my family more in how I choose to prioritise my time?

If you can't answer this question from within yourself, then don't do what you're thinking of doing until you can. Even if your answer may be destructive to your brand and to trust, and you decide to do it after having answered the question, at least you've answered for the sake of what. You will, of course, have to take responsibility for and live with the consequences of your choice and the action that followed.

By habitually asking yourself this question, you will be more trusted by others and your relationships will be stronger. You will consider others as much as, if not more than, yourself.

As I shared at the top of this chapter, this question is also core to your ability to ground your assessments.

You might say, "Is that all there is to it? Ask myself 'for the sake of what/whom?' and people will trust me?" No. People will trust you when you continuously deliver on your commitments. However, by asking yourself this question before you do or say anything, you will hold yourself accountable for your actions, be it in deed or in language. This will bring about more legitimising of self and that will build trust by others. If you ask yourself after the deed or use of language, "for the sake of what/whom did I do that?", that will help you be a learner and take action or use language more effectively next time.

Are there any exceptions? I'm not sure there are, to be honest. Ask yourself why asking this question is not possible. I'm not sure you'll find many reasons, but if you do, then I'd love to know.

So, ask yourself #FTSOW before you take your next action, both in deed and in language. The only barrier to you doing this consciously is remembering to do it if you make the choice to do it. As a client of mine has done, perhaps you could write #FTSOW on one of your hands.

Trust and the 'Commitment Cycle' - stage one

I am only sharing stage one of the four stages of the cycle with you here, as this is the stage that is related to your Way of Doing. The other three are related to both yours and another person's Way of Doing, and we will cover them in chapter six.

The commitment cycle is fundamental to your Way of Doing and delivering on your commitment to self and others. It's a way of using language to ensure that your requests and offers are trustworthy, as the model contains elements of the Seven Assessments of Trust (being invested in another's concerns, sincerity, vulnerability, competence, capacity and reliability), which we talked about in chapter one. It's a way of taking action to ensure that both you and the other party deliver on your and their commitments consistently.

Stage one of the commitment cycle is making the request. Alan Sieler, in *Coaching to the Human Soul volume one*, provides a model called "making and managing commitments". He shares that, "Making and managing commitments are at the heart of how our lives function and are central to the performance and productivity of organisations. Thousands upon thousands of requests and promises are made in organisations every day. Coordinating action can be viewed as a cycle." Trust is either built or lost throughout that cycle.

For example, I'll ask you to meet me for a coffee at the local cafe this morning. Unless I let you know which local cafe and at what time, then it's not a highly effective request. The importance of how we make a request is fundamental to the initiation of the trust process in this domain of language. We make requests of others so often in a day that we actually lose count.

The Commitment Cycle

1 Making the request
- Competency
- Capacity
- Standard
- Timeline
- Clarity
- Consequence
- Concerns

Gaining a commitment on the request 2
Options:
- Yes
- No
- Clarify and negotiate
- Commit to commit later
- Slippery promise

4 Assessing the request Trust

OK	Not OK
· Appreciate	· Why
· Recognise	· How to fix
	· Next steps

Delivering on the request 3
- Do it
- Provide updates:
  - good
  - bad
- Renegotiate (if required)

Adapted from Alan Sieler *Coaching to the Human Soul volume one*

Here are the components to the initial stage of the commitment cycle. The first stage is all about setting you up for success by making an effective request and setting up for success the person you are making the request of.

Ila Edgar and Charles Feltman on their podcast *Trust on Purpose* ask you to consider this – are you making the request yourself, or on behalf of someone else? This is a great addition to the set-up for making a request, as there will be times when you will have to make a request of someone on behalf of someone else. If this is the case, please ensure you have got the context, and clarity, from that person which will enable you to make an effective request, based on what I am about to share with you.

You need to know what needs to be done in your request. Does the person have the competency to carry out the request? Does the person have the capacity to carry out the request? To what standard are you making the request? In what timeline do you want the request to be done? Do you know what the consequence will be of this person not delivering on the request? And, if so, do they? Finally, what might their concerns be?

Be clear on what is to be done, provide clarity and consequence, and accept that clarity may be requested by the person whom you are making the request of – especially if there are concerns for that person in your request. Be open to it.

Think about the competency first. This will be an assessment of whether the person you are making the request of has the competency to carry out the request. As a leader, you should know this. If you don't, ask the question of the person you are assessing to help you ascertain if this is the case or not. When it comes to capacity, this must never be underestimated. The person may have the competency, however because of what you have loaded that person up with yesterday, last week or last month, do they have the current capacity to carry out your request? Part of this assessment is being invested in their concerns – their own competency and/or capacity could be a concern of theirs. Again, this is an assessment that you will have to make. If you're not sure, ask them.

To what standard are you making the request? By standard, I mean the standard that you believe is appropriate for what you've laid out as your standards of behaviour or work in any context, and what the accepted standard is in your business. (If you're working to raise the standard as a leader, then make your request in line with that higher standard.)

With time, be precise. If you mean by Friday lunchtime, say Friday lunchtime. If any time Friday is okay, then make that clear. Provide clarity, which partly comes from the previous two points of standard and time. However, don't assume they have clarity. Ask the person you are making the request of if they are clear on your request. Part of this action will be you considering what your relationship is with this person – how will they feel about asking for clarity? Will they have to be vulnerable and courageous to seek clarity? If so, recognise that and make it easier for them to do so.

Does the person know the consequence of not delivering on their commitment? As Brian Hartzer says in his book *The Leadership Star*, "without consequences for failure, the value of clarity will fall, along with engagement". Remember, both parties can agree on what the consequences are of not delivering on the request.

Finally, ask if they have any concerns with your request. These concerns may not be evident to you, or shared by the person, so give them the opportunity to share them by asking them the question.

This also works when it comes to making an offer. You have to deliver on your commitment made in that offer to create trust.

Ask yourself these questions and also relate them to the elements of the Seven Assessments of Trust:

- Do I have the competency and capacity to deliver on my offer reliably (both standard and time)?
- Is my offer clear?
- Do I have your best interests at heart when I make this offer to you? Am I invested in your concerns and am I sincere in that?
- Am I aware of the consequences of not delivering on my offer?
- Do I have any concerns about this offer that I am making?

These are questions for you to answer before you make an offer. Also ask yourself, "For the sake of what/whom am I making this offer? Is it more about me and my concerns, or is it to take care of the other person's concerns?" If it is the former, then don't make the offer.

Ultimately, whether delivering on an offer you make, or you delivering on a request that someone makes of you, will create or break trust depending on how well you do that task and deliver on your commitment. We'll talk more about this in the next chapter too.

As a leader, this cycle relates directly to your leadership style and the culture of your organisation. Think of how many requests you have already made today. Can you count how many requests you made yesterday? Now think of how many offers you have made. The balance of offers versus requests made by leaders can say so much about you, your leadership style, and the culture (or mood) of your organisation. Are you a leader who only makes requests and is your organisation constantly making requests and very few offers? If so, think of what's happening down at the lower levels of management and on the 'shop floor'.

These requests tumble down through layers of management. The folk 'at the bottom' get swamped and have no support (in terms of offers) made to them. I've worked in organisations like that, and I'm not proud to say that at times I've led like that. It doesn't end well. These questions of self are the start to creating the bond of trust, through the effective use of language, when asking someone to do something for you. If you cannot answer all of these seven elements of an effective request/offer then don't make the initial request, or don't make the offer as it will lead to a diminution of trust.

You may say it's just too hard to do this every time I ask someone to do something for me. Really? I don't think so. Asking yourself, "For the sake of what am I making this request?" and then asking the questions above is not that hard. It does, however, take a level of consciousness, self-awareness and practice – that's the hard bit. But isn't it worth it, asking these questions of yourself to get a better outcome and build trust? It reminds me of the six Ps saying, "Prior Planning Prevents Piss Poor Performance." This is a deeper way of preventing piss poor performance in those you make a request of. It begins with you.

When you don't make an effective request, you should forgive yourself and learn from it. In chapter six, we'll talk about making an assessment of how well the request has been delivered on by the other person, and what role forgiveness can play there too.

You may say there's a difference in language between a request where the receiver has options – which we'll talk about in chapter six – and an instruction. As written in dictionary.com a request is, "the act of asking for something to be given or done, especially as a favor or courtesy" and instructing is "to furnish with orders or directions". Yes, there are fundamental differences. However, the assessments of competency, capacity and ensuring clarity of standard and time, and knowing the consequences are all applicable to an instruction as well as a request. I acknowledge you may not ask about the concerns of the other in making an instruction. Without this, trust is on a slippery slope. In both cases, trust is an outcome of delivering on the request or the instruction.

Practical application

When thinking about your recent requests, were you clear on what time and standard your request needed to meet? Did you accept that the person you made the request of has the option to ask for clarity or negotiate? Did the person have the capacity and competency to complete your request? Did you outline the consequences of not delivering? Did you consider their concerns? Analyse your requests relative to these questions. How effective have your requests been according to these criteria? If you score low, think about how you're creating the environment of trust for those who work for you, who you work with and who you work for, and for the person you're in a relationship with (if you are). For one week, take note of every request and every offer you make. Record this in two columns on a sheet of paper or in a spreadsheet. At the end of the week, look at the ledger. What assessment do you make of it? Once you've made that assessment, what choices do you have? When you've thought about your choices of potentially redressing the balance, what action are you going to take? This is another example of my Observe|Choose|Act framework in action, when relating to requests and offers.

The barrier you may face here is making time to do this before every request. Make the time, because it will be well invested over the length of the commitment cycle and save time in the long run. Think of the Covey model of trust – balancing time and costs – which I shared with you early in the book. This is applicable in taking the time to make an effective request. It will lead to less time overall in the commitment cycle and, if appropriate to the request, a lower cost. If that doesn't work for you, think of the 6 Ps!

Trust and 'types of conversations'

Every time we speak with someone, it is a conversation. As such, every conversation we have can be labelled as a type of conversation.

When you converse with someone there are 'four people in your conversation'.

Four people in a conversation

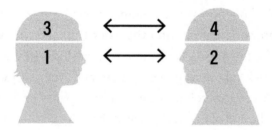

Think of it this way – when looking at the illustration above, you are the odd numbers and the other person is the even numbers. In many cases only 'person one' and 'person two' are having a conversation audibly. In other words 'person three' and 'person four' (the internal listening or dialogue in our heads) are not engaged (picture someone on their phone when you are talking to them). A truly effective conversation is when persons three and four 'talk through' persons one and two, then you will be 'talking to the other person's listening'. When you do this there is alignment between what you are both thinking and saying.

How do you do this? Firstly, hold them as 'the legitimate other', and then secondly ask questions while in a mood of curiosity to understand their story and 'where they are coming from'. If you can do that, the next part of the book will be so much more effective.

To ensure every conversation has a purpose and outcome, put a label on it. A conversation creates a new reality for those who partake in that conversation.

Types of Conversations

#FTSOW ➡ **TOC** ⟶ KPI

Here's a statement to consider: "we walk in and out of every conversation". What do I mean by this? Look at the diagram above and think of every conversation as a circle with at least you and one other person in it. You may also think of it as a room with a door at either end of the room. You walk into and out of every conversation. If you don't, then you'll be talking to that same person for the rest of your life! Every conversation has a beginning and an end. I do acknowledge that not everyone can physically walk, so please see this as entering and exiting a room if that helps.

"For the sake of what am I having or going to have this conversation?" We've covered this earlier in the chapter. Before any conversation you have, ask yourself, "#FTSOW am I having, or am I going to have this conversation?" Think of this as the broad domain of why you are going to have the conversation (hence the broader arrow going into the circle). The next question to ask yourself before you have the conversation is, "What is my definition of success for this conversation? What is my KPI?" The answer to this question needs to be more specific, hence the narrowness of the arrow coming out in the diagram. You might say 'laser like'. You note these two arrows are on the same plain in the diagram. It is critical that there is alignment between your #FTSOW and your KPI – if they are not aligned it will not be a successful conversation. Once you've answered these questions, you can put a label on the type of conversation you're about to have.

Let's put a label to these 10 'types of conversations':

1. **Stories and personal assessments.** This is where you share your views and stories with others. Most of our social conversations are of this type. Core to this type of conversation is listening to where the other person is coming from, their story, and holding them as 'the legitimate other'. It is also an opportunity to ask people to share 'what are you thinking?', as well as 'what are you feeling?' This latter question is critical to how you will be able to lead more effectively in today's rapidly changing commercial world. As you will have realised, I am sure, by

asking in the domain of feeling, you are asking a question of the person's 'way of being'. The KPI to this could be, "I simply want to understand more about where you're coming from, what you're thinking and feeling on the matter without holding any judgement." Another KPI could simply be, "we are both heard", or "Ubuntu" (I see you). In a team environment, if you choose to create this type of conversation as a leader, there are only two 'rules' really – one is to ensure everyone listens and the second is not to judge, but to be curious as to where the person who is talking is 'coming from' in their story telling. Both 'rules' are fundamental to holding each person in the room as 'the legitimate other'.

2. **Possibilities and opportunities.** This is where you speculate about future possibilities – you could also call this brainstorming. The distinction between possibilities and opportunities is where you or the group believe the opportunity can be created into a plan of action. Core to this type of conversation is being curious. The KPI here could be coming up with a number of possibilities that you break down into real opportunities to work on at another time.

3. **Clarity.** This is where you have clarity on something you hear, or you want to clarify something you've said to another to confirm their listening or understanding. As a leader this is where you can make the distinction in language between someone's "priorities" and someone's "concerns". I have shared with you already the ontological notion of "concerns" (something that deeply matters to you), so in a conversation for clarity you can ask what a

person's priorities are, however that may not cover off all their concerns. As you know, in business you will have several priorities. Let's say a person in your team has four priorities; I am sure that not all of them will be 'concerns' for that person. Maybe only one of them will be, the other three they know will be delivered. If you don't get clarity on someone's concerns (as well as their priorities), you may miss what is really holding them back from delivering on their commitments. This could be something to do with a relationship at work, at home or something else that will not be covered off by you gaining clarity, as a leader, solely on their priorities.

Core to this type of conversation is consciously listening and asking questions. The KPI here is that you both end up on the same page and confirm this is so.

4. **Action or the coordination of action.** This is where you get the list of who's doing what that must lead to public and audible declarations, requests, offers and commitments being made. The KPI here is that you and the other person, or your team, have openly declared and committed to a course of action where each person has clarity on their action. You have collectively agreed this is the right course of action and each person is committed to their personal action.

5. **Accountability and common commitment.** This is especially relevant after a public declaration has been made in the domain of a team where individuals have openly declared a commitment to a course of action. The KPI here is that you ensure there is clear accountability for who is doing what, especially

Trust your Way of Doing

after a public declaration has been made in the team environment. A RACI (responsible, accountable, consult, inform) is typically done in this type of conversation.

6. **Progress.** A subset of a conversation for clarity, where you ask, "How's the person progressing?" It's also an opportunity to offer to support their progress. The KPI here is that you are updated on how something or someone is tracking in regard to their commitment made to you, or how you are going with your commitment made to a person when you made an offer. This conversation is core to stage three of the commitment cycle, as you will read later in the book.

7. **Accomplishment.** This is where you make a public acknowledgement of *what has been accomplished or achieved*. This is more about the task. The KPI here is going public and acknowledging the accomplishment of the task to the standard and time agreed.

8. **Appreciation and recognition.** This is an opportunity to appreciate progress, where you make a public recognition that you appreciate *what the person has done and how they've delivered* that on their commitments. This is more humanistic. It's about the person or the team. The KPI here is you appreciating or recognising the person or team delivering on their commitment.

9. **Performance.** A conversation where you make it clear that the person or team is not performing to the standard expected and, most importantly, the standard agreed in the commitment cycle. The KPI here is that the person has clarity on what you assess is the failure of their performance against the commitment made,

129

both to a standard and a time. Please don't use the 'sandwich technique' (cushioning performance feedback with positive feedback) and leave the person confused and asking, "Was I just spoken to about substandard performance?" That's no good for you or for them.

Also, please don't label this type of conversation as 'difficult'. What is a 'difficult conversation'? Who is it 'difficult' for? How well does it serve you to label it a 'difficult conversation'? Even by asking these three questions, I hope it brings you to a place where you hear yourself say, "perhaps this is not a great place to start when I think of having 'that' conversation!"

Labelling something as 'difficult', or perhaps 'hard', can arguably serve you well – it can make you focus, it can enable you to prepare, it can make you think about what you are going to do, how you are going to do it, what you say, and why you are going to say it. However, in my experience when it comes to these types of conversations, this is rarely the case. What happens is, as soon as you label a conversation as 'difficult', it usually closes you up to possibilities of how to have the conversation and why you should have the conversation. Typically, we come from a mood of anxiety when we label a conversation as 'difficult', and as such we don't prepare, we leave it to the last minute, or worse still we avoid even having it.

Given this advice, you might try using the SBI Feedback Model, created by the Centre for Creative Leadership, that refers to "Situation, Behaviour, Impact". This is put brilliantly by Genevieve Hawkins in her book *Mentally at Work*, where she writes about each of these areas in great detail to support you giving feedback as a leader. Here is a vignette of each from her book:

- Situation – "it's essential to give a specific time and location when providing feedback to someone."
- Behaviour – "give specific, observable actions rather than assumptions of what you think is going on in that person's emotions."
- Impact – "The impact is about the effect on you. Essentially you are telling the person what happened in the classroom inside your head". ("Classroom inside your head" is a phrase she uses throughout her book to describe your brain, your thoughts, and your emotions – note the common theme here?).

I add to this SBI model, 'D' and 'C':

- Differently – "what can the person do differently next time?" You can either ask them or instruct them.
- Commitment – "ensure you receive a commitment from the person that they will do what they said they were going to do differently."

In this type of conversation, you can change the model to be 'SPIDC', where it is related to performance (situation/performance/impact/differently/commitment) to focus on being specific about a performance shortfall. In this type of conversation (i.e. for performance) you must treat the person as 'the legitimate other' and your mood must be appropriate for the conversation, as shared earlier in this chapter.

I was sharing this type of conversation and 'the legitimate other' with a client recently, and that leader said he used a person's brand to have this type of conversation.

The technique of using a person's brand came from this leader caring about how the person receiving the performance feedback is perceived by peers/colleagues. He asks the person, "are you aware of how people perceive you?" He ensures that he has examples of his own impressions as well as others' impressions. This can be a very effective way of using a third party, as well as yourself, to share performance feedback, while still coming from a place of care. This executive leader found in many cases that the person receiving the feedback was not aware of their brand and how others see them. Given this, they found it very useful to know, and then do something about it.

However, the person still needs to understand that they are not performing to the required standard and what your expectations and consequences are going forward. That is ultimately your responsibility in this type of conversation.

I acknowledge this can be a courageous conversation for you, however please don't label it as 'difficult' for the reasons I have outlined.

You can also use this SBI technique in a 'conversation for appreciation and recognition' too.

10. **Relationship** (both working and personal). The focus in this conversation is about the relationship between yourself and the other person. It could be about wanting to build on a new relationship or a recurrent breakdown in how you are getting on, or how you are feeling about the relationship. Action that you have individually taken has not resulted in desired improvements. This is a public acknowledgement that the relationship is not going

well by at least one party. It could also be a facilitated conversation for working relationships between two others by someone else. The KPI here is ensuring that any issue in your relationship is addressed and that you both leave the conversation feeling the relationship is better than it was before the conversation was held, or at least that you have shared your feelings on the relationship to try to improve it.

Again, you can use the SBI(DC) model here, if it is the behaviour in the relationship that you want to draw attention to.

The basis of this model is an adaptation of Alan Sieler's *Coaching to the Human Soul, volume one.*

I hear you say, surely there are more than 10 types of conversations? I certainly did when I was first introduced to this by Alan Sieler in my coach training. However, in the work that I now do with leaders using this model, these 10 conversations seem to cover all bases. Please let me know if there's a type of conversation you have that isn't in one of these 10. I'd love to know about that as I'm a learner too.

You might be concerned that it's a bit formulaic to see every conversation in this light – having a purpose and a KPI and then labelling it. It depends on how heavily you hold the purpose and KPI. For example, if you are having a conversation with your mates or your family, are you likely to do these pre-assessments? Probably not. However, knowing that most conversations in this domain are for stories and assessments, all you need to consider is how you hold the other person as 'the legitimate other', how consciously you listen, and if you are in a mood of curiosity. If not, then you will not get the KPI you're looking for – which in this case is probably to be comfortable in that person's company and feel good about the conversation and the time spent together. Building on this notion of 'the legitimate other' and you not getting your KPI – did the other person get what they wanted from the conversation? If so, that may be enough for you to 'park' that conversation and go back to it another day to 'hit' yours.

Surely there are a number of different conversations that are taking place at the same time? This is possible and, to be honest, probable – especially without these distinctions – which is why you leave so many conversations asking yourself, "What on earth was that all about? What did we achieve there?" I have tried to illustrate this very real possibility with the interlocking circles in the illustration on page 125, that depict multiple types of conversations occurring within one overall 'type of conversation'. The trick is to make an assessment about where you are in that conversation. If you can, pull it back into the space of your #FTSOW and your KPI to keep it on track. If it's someone else's conversation that you find yourself in, ask them the question of #FTSOW and what their KPI is.

Another tip to having effective conversations is to sequence your conversations so that they each have a purpose and an outcome, rather than trying to cover everything at once. This can be done over an extended period – you might want to see it as a 'strategic series of conversations' to get an outcome over weeks, or even months, with your boss, a client, a supplier or even your team.

Practical application

Here's an example of where I've done this. In my Coaching Practice, I've facilitated Board strategy days, using the sequencing of 'types of conversations' as the agenda for the day. The agenda looked something like this:

1. Stories and assessments. Let's get our thoughts on the table about where the business is at and legitimise them by hearing them, not judging them or each other.
2. Progress, accomplishment and recognition. The CEO updates the Board on where the business is at since the last strategy session. (This will include some stories and assessments based on the presenting of assessments (beliefs) and assertions (data/facts) by the CEO.)
3. Possibilities and opportunities. Co-creating thoughts as a Board for what the business/CEO might want to consider in the next year to 18 months.
4. Coordination of action and agreement on the next steps.
5. Commitment. Each Board member and the CEO commits to individual declarations made about the next steps.
6. Stories and assessments again. Why? That was the drinks after the strategy day!

This is something you can try with your team if you are having a strategy or an 'away day'.

Every conversation you have is a 'type of conversation'. The only exception might be if you can come up with a conversation that can't fit into one of these 10 distinctions. If so, I'd love to hear about it.

Consider the notion that you 'walk in and out of every conversation'. Think about your #FTSOW and what your KPI is before you walk into any conversation. I've asked you to consider asking yourself these questions when you are in someone else's conversation to help keep it or that person on track. #FTSOW do I ask you to do this? Because it works. You will coordinate action and be trusted more than you are now, even if you know or assess that you're already highly trusted.

It takes time and practice. Think about the six Ps. That's reason enough to do it, isn't it?

Trust and your brand and reputation

This part is about your brand and how it relates to your Way of Doing.

Your brand and reputation are core to how people see you and what you're known for. Your brand and reputation are in large part based on how you deliver on your commitments. The outcome of this is trust, so therefore your brand and reputation are directly associated with trust. I already have shared with you how your brand (or another person's brand) can be directly related to your performance.

I've compared Trump with Mandela when introducing ego versus legacy. Now consider the brand and reputation of Michael Jordan. In 2020 he appeared in the Netflix series 'The Last Dance'. Having no opinion of him prior to watching the series, after viewing it I would say that his brand typifies deep and shallow ambition – refer to the Moods Framework in chapter four – and delivering on his commitments, both to himself and others around him. I do acknowledge that some commentators and peers interviewed in the series found his Way of Being and Doing very self-serving and not 'for others'. This assessment can be grounded, I am sure, however in my view this is balanced by what he brought to the team and how he coached and mentored others to raise their standards. He had the courage to follow his dream into the NBA after being told he was too short to play at varsity level and to continue playing at the highest level after his father was killed in 1993. He had both the patience and perseverance to carry on playing between his first three NBA titles (1991, 1992 and 1993) and his second three titles (1996, 1997, 1998), even after taking a break to play baseball.

He showed his passion and enthusiasm in that time, after returning to the game from playing baseball in 1995. His reputation is, according to an ESPN survey of journalists in 1999, that he is, "the greatest North American athlete of the 20th century (greater than Ali)" and in 1999 the associated press voted him "the greatest basketball player of the 20th century". His brand will always be associated with Nike for his Air Jordan shoes launched in 1984, as confirmed in the *Business Insider* magazine in May 2019. He would not be this iconic figure in the minds of the public if he did not deliver on his commitment of 'making it happen'. He is quoted as saying, "Some people want it to happen. Some wish it would happen. Others make it happen." *(Ref Steven R. Covey tweet May 2019)*

Surely your brand and reputation are more than delivering on your commitments? Well, yes. It's based on another's assessment of your experience, expertise, competencies and actions/ performance in a community or market. It will also include how you portray your beliefs, what your conduct is and your behaviour when related to societal expectations in societies where you predominantly present yourself. Let's break down some of these accepted attributes of your brand and relate them to what I've shared with you about trusting your Way of Doing (and Being).

We've covered 'expertise' and 'competencies' in the commitment cycle, where someone will make an assessment before asking you to do something based on these attributes. 'Portray your beliefs' – we covered this in chapter two, about your stories and how you present them to others. With regards to your conduct and behaviour think about your own standards, how you set them and how you deliver against them when delivering on a request or offer or take action either in deed or in language. These will all relate directly to your brand and reputation.

Relate your brand to the Seven Assessments of Trust: your *vulnerability*, including to others' actions, you being *invested* in another's concerns, your *sincerity* in this, your *reliability*, your *competence*, your *capacity* and that you do all this *consistently*.

The only aspect of brand related to trust that has not been covered by my book is your experience. I accept this is possibly an exception. However, make no mistake, people will make an assessment on your experience as to whether they trust you.

As evidence of this, based on my brand and reputation, someone suggested that a person seek me out for Executive Coaching. This person chose to assess my experience, coach training and competency before engaging me. He asked me how many hours of coaching experience I had undertaken when he was considering my coaching proposal, what coach credentials I have, as well as the types of organisations that I had coached leaders in and for testimonials/references. This is a classic example of my brand and reputation being assessed by my experience and competency before this person chose to trust me as his Executive Coach.

Yes, these are all assessments related to your brand and reputation, however when it all comes down to it, your brand and reputation are inextricably linked to you consistently delivering on your commitments. They will be assessed by the way in which you do it (being vulnerable, being invested and your sincerity in that), how you consistently deliver on your commitments (behaviour and conduct), to what standard (training, competency and capacity), and the deadline you say you will do it by (reliability). These core assessments combine elements of both your Way of Being and your Way of Doing when related to your brand and reputation.

I said in chapter four I would come back to a potential incongruence between the mood you are in and the way you may 'need' to present yourself in a certain situation if you are in a 'below the line mood', which is related to the brand others observe. I am not sure there is such an incongruence – by observing your mood in the first place, that is starting to reduce the incongruence because you are acknowledging it. By finding the 'right' energy, or emotion (which is short term) to lead in that situation you further dispel the incongruence, because you are present in the moment with the 'right' energy to lead in that moment in time. For sure, you may well have to visit the underlying mood that you find yourself in later in the day, however that is in the process of observing your mood and then choosing to take the action to shift it.

Practical application

Ask yourself, "What is my brand and reputation?" An easy way to do that is ask yourself these two questions: "How am I seen?" and "What am I known for?" This will help you to answer what your brand and reputation is. In 2020, I asked these questions openly for others to answer about me on a LinkedIn post. It was both illuminating and humbling to get the responses that I did. I'll tell you, it took courage and vulnerability to do it. Even if you can answer them, you should ask them as well to verify or ground your assessment of yourself.

The greatest barrier is facing into the fact (an assertion) that you have a brand. Once you're at peace with this fact, you may be able to be curious. Note the moods framework here and think about what mood might predispose you to be able to ask others what your brand is. This will take courage and vulnerability to do this. However, it will be worth it. It was for me.

You may be asking yourself, "#FTSOW should I do this?" It's to find out what your brand and reputation is, to learn from it, to consider choices, to take action, to improve it, and hopefully to be more trusted. Again, this is another example of my framework of Observe|Choose|Act, this time in the domain of brand and reputation.

Trust and being in flow

Being in flow is the intersection in my model and New Ordering of Trust, between Way of Being and Way of Doing. It is where you will be at your best in consistently delivering on your commitments, trusting yourself, and being trusted by others.

According to Steven Kotler, *New York Times* bestselling author and an award-winning journalist and the Executive Director of the Flow Research Collective, "Flow is defined as an optimal state of consciousness, a state where you feel your best and perform your best. More specifically, the term refers to those moments of rapt attention and total absorption, when you get so focused on the task at hand that everything else disappears. Action and awareness merge. Your sense of self vanishes. Your sense of time distorts (either, typically, speeds up; or, occasionally, slows down). And throughout, all aspects of performance, both mental and physical, go through the roof." *(Stevenkotler.com)*

Kotler paints a great picture above. I would say, being in flow is where the magic happens in life. This is where people will choose to follow you and will trust you because you are living authentically. You are in your natural state. When you are doing, you are doing in a state of being that enables you to be seemingly effortless in how you take action and deliver on your commitments. It comes from your Way of Being and transcends into your Way of Doing. That's why it's placed at the intersection of these two domains in my New Ordering of Trust.

One of my stories of being in flow is when I was caddying for Ben, the Pennant player who I caddy for at my golf club. Without going into too much detail, the possibility of losing the golf match was high, when he stood on the 17th tee (out of 18). Something happened where, even in a very difficult situation, standing at the back of the 17th green, with his ball next to a bush and us watching his opponent in the bunker, we both had this 'sixth sense' at the same time, that he wasn't going to lose the match there and then, or at all. There was trust in each other as we were both in flow in that moment deciding the options. Ben won that hole against the odds, with a superb shot and ended up tying the match on the last hole. I can't describe what happened, but we both felt something at the same time standing by that bush, which in a later conversation with me, he shared that he felt the same.

Mihaly Csikszentmihalyi is known for his research on the 'experience of flow', a psychological concept he introduced in his bestselling book *Flow: The Psychology of Optimal Experience* (Harper Perennial, 1990). According to PositivePsychology.com his work is known for eight characteristics of flow, all of which I have chosen to match against my model and New Ordering of Trust in italics:

1. Complete concentration on the task – *'Being present in your Way of Doing'*

2. Clarity of goals and reward in mind and immediate feedback – #FTSOW and *Commitment cycle*

3. Transformation of time (speeding up/slowing down) – *Noticing your physiology and energy*

4. The experience is intrinsically rewarding – *Noticing your physiology, mood and the language you use to describe it, either to self or others*

5. Effortlessness and ease – *'My Flow' as per Ennis Hill/ Hamilton (see below)*

6. There is a balance between challenge and skills – *your mood of ambition and your capability to deliver on it*

7. Actions and awareness are merged, losing self-conscious rumination – *Taking action in Observe|Choose|Act and linking that action with flow*

8. There is a feeling of control over the task – *knowing your #FTSOW and being in a mood of deep ambition (courage, patience and perseverance)*

In Csikszentmihalyi's words, flow is "a state in which people are so involved in an activity that nothing else seems to matter; the experience is so enjoyable that people will continue to do it even at great cost, for the sheer sake of doing it" (1990). *(PositivePsychology.com)*

I look to the sporting world where the person has personally alluded to this notion by quoting them to demonstrate what I mean. Lewis Hamilton, a Formula One World Champion and arguably the greatest driver that has ever lived, said after the August 2020 Spanish Grand Prix and quoted on the BBC Formula One website that, "There is an immense amount of pressure on us all to perform weekend-in, weekend-out … And in the chase for perfection and being in that zone, you can be very, very close, but still slightly out and not quite be in your perfect rhythm … But for whatever reason today, I can't quite pinpoint why, I feel like I was in the most … It was like a clear zone." This is what I'm talking about. His Way of Being met his Way of Doing to create a dominant victory on that day, and at that time he was only three F1 race wins behind Michael Schumacher. His notion of being 'in the zone' is what I'm referring to as being in flow. He has now overtaken Schumacher's record of 94 wins at the time of writing and now equalled his record of seven titles.

To stay with a sporting theme, Jessica Ennis-Hill, who won the heptathlon in the 2012 London Olympics and was "the face of the games", is quoted as saying, "My idea of beauty is somebody that doesn't have to try too much. Someone who is effortless and fresh." On the first day of her event, she set two personal bests and had her highest first-day score ever. On day two, she set another personal best and won the final event, the 800 metres, when there was actually no need for her to do so to win the gold medal, as she was so far ahead in the points. She was in flow with her performance over those two days and her quote reflects this. She looked 'effortless and fresh'. However, as we all know, she was trying her hardest for herself, for the team, and for the whole British nation. Looking at this from a 'Way of Being' meeting a 'Way of Doing', they omnipotently met for Ennis-Hill on those two days in August 2012.

You may say, "I am no Hamilton, Ennis-Hill or Jordan." That's true. However, you do have both a Way of Being and a Way of Doing that it is possible to bring together in such a way that you are in flow. Think of it as 'through me', using Jim Dethmer's four states of consciousness model, shared through the Conscious Leadership Group in a Coaches Rising *Transformative Presence* session.

Here are the four states of consciousness in his model, with his words in quotes and my interpretation of each:

- 'To me' is someone or something doing something to me. In Dethmer's words, "I am at the effect of". "The person is a victim to people or circumstances around them and they may feel threatened, they blame, or feel helpless". You may ask in this context, am I below the line (using the moods framework) and in opposition or disempowered because someone or something is doing something 'to me' that I feel I can't control?

- 'By me' is where you are conscious of your Way of Doing, or a 'creator of your own experience'. In this state you really have to focus and think about what you are doing and you take responsibility for your actions. It just doesn't seem natural and may seem a bit forced. I'm sure both Hamilton and Ennis-Hill have felt this at times in training and where they've not competed at their best, even if they won on that day.

- 'Through me' is where you are in flow, where nobody's doing anything to you and you're not thinking too hard or making what you are doing 'by me'. Here "people surrender their own personal agenda and begin to collaborate with an awareness greater than themselves". It is a state of being where what you are doing or even saying is 'through you'. You feel in flow.

- 'As me' will be covered in the last chapter of the book as it is more spiritual in nature and not directly relevant here.

Practical application

Using the Dethmer's model above, take note of when you are in a 'through me' state of consciousness, as opposed to 'to me' or 'by me' – a distinction of you being in flow. At a more existential level, simply notice when you feel in a state where your Way of Being in all three domains (language, moods, physiology) is aligned to your Way of Doing. Take note afterwards of where you were and what you were doing. What can you learn from this experience?

#FTSOW am I asking you to do this? So that you can be in flow more often by observing yourself in that state. By doing this, trust within and around you will grow.

This observation of being in flow is not easy and it's easiest done after you've experienced the feeling. If you can notice it in the moment, great. However, that will take some practise.

Conclusion

You've been introduced to the self-accountability question of #FTSOW, which leads directly to you trusting yourself and the outcome of others trusting you. I've shared the first stage of the commitment cycle, which is a way in language to ensure you make effective requests and offers. I have shared with you the notion that every conversation you have is a 'type of conversation' and that by knowing this, you will communicate and listen more effectively, coordinate action more effectively, lead more effectively, and ultimately be trusted more through your use of language.

I've taken you through how your brand and reputation are inextricably linked with trust and how you can find out what your brand is by asking two questions. Finally, I've shared with you the notion of being 'in flow', which I determine in my New Ordering of Trust to be the intersection of your Way of Being aligning with your Way of Doing.

The barriers you may face in trusting your Way of Doing are all in your Way of Being and your Way of Doing. You have choices, whether or not you take action in this domain. Observe your Way of Doing and make the choice to ask others about their assessment of it. Then take action on what you assess needs changing in your Way of Doing.

#FTSOW, you might ask. For others to trust you more and for you to trust yourself more. In essence, this is achieved using the Observe|Choose|Act framework, as related to your Way of Doing.

What's coming up?

Coming up in the next chapter is placing your trust in others and how that relates to both your Way of Being and your Way of Doing.

Six

Trust in others

CO'M model and Ordering of Trust

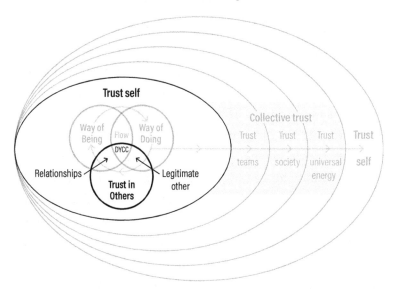

We now move out of the 'me' part of the trust model and into the 'you' part of it. To trust others, you must legitimise them and be appropriately vulnerable and prepared to be vulnerable to their actions. In this chapter, I will introduce you fully to 'the legitimate other' and share the remaining three elements of the commitment cycle. They're in this section because they inherently involve trusting others.

Relationships are the intersection between trusting others and trusting your Way of Being. This is an outcome of trusting the other person, or people, as well as your Way of Being and your Way of Doing. To have a strong relationship, you must both consistently deliver on your commitments and have each other's concerns in your heart – i.e. be sincerely invested in their concerns. You want to take care of what matters to them and trust that they are in the relationship to take care of your concerns and what really matters to you. The heart of the model is you both consistently delivering on your commitment to yourself and to others.

Trust, when it comes to trusting another, is at least a two-way street. I hope by now you see it is more than that, however, it is undeniably at least two-way. You and me. I must explore the other person in the trust dynamic with you for us to bring this topic to any conclusion. If we only see trust as about me – Am I trustworthy? Do I trust myself? – then we're missing the point. Without completing the cycle of trust in language, you will miss the opportunity to see how the commitment cycle can help you lead and coordinate action more effectively, as well as building trust in self and between you and others. How we see the other person, and what we want to trust and be trusted by, are crucial to the trust equation. Are you legitimising the person? Trust is at the heart of any strong relationship between two or more people.

A commonly used model for trusting others is the 'Three circles of trust', based on "**community** – the lowest form of trust with those you consider acquaintances"; "**crowd** – a deeper level of trust based on personal knowledge of the person and a demonstration of trust such that the behaviour can be predicted over time"; "**core** – the innermost circle reserved for the closest of friends, family and life partner, characterised by knowing the hopes, dreams, fears, and insecurities of each other" – Randy Conley, leading with trust.com. I do acknowledge this model and how it may serve you if you know it and use it, however I feel it does not go to the essence of what it means to trust another, regardless of how well you know them or not. This is a societal perspective that seems to hang on the type of commitment made and how sincere you are in investing in another's concerns (from not personal to deeply personal). In my view, it doesn't take into account 'the legitimate other' regardless of how well you know them, nor the Seven Assessments of Trust, or one's own Way of Being and Way of Doing. I recently had a conversation with a CEO on this distinction, where I was asked about the distinction of 'being invested in another's concerns' and 'being sincere' in that. I shared that it is possible to see trust at different levels, as this model implies, however at its core if you are vulnerable and vulnerable to another's actions, are invested in another person's concerns and are sincere in that, that is where the essence of trust lies, in 'your way of being'. I do accept though that the concerns of a person that you invest yourself in from a professional per-spective do differ from the concerns you invest yourself in when in a personal relationship. This is arguably the distinction that Conley is making, using an ontological perspective to assess it by.

I know I'm going to be at the café I've asked you to meet me at on time. However, I'm quite sure, based on our previous experi-ence, that you're going to be late. I decide to finish writing this chapter before I meet you, knowing that I might be 10 minutes late. I assess that this is okay because you are always late. I will not let you know that I'm running late. However, this time you're on time and I'm not. You've held me as 'the legitimate other' but I have not held you in the same way. I've put myself first based on my assessment that you're going to be late. Your trust in me has taken a bit of a hit because you made sure that you're on time, knowing that I'm always on time. I do want to acknowledge that in some cultures, arriving between 5 and 15 minutes within the appointed time may not be assessed in the same way with regards to respecting or legitimising the other person.

This example came to mind because someone recently shared with me, "Mate, you're like a Swiss watch when it comes to being on time." How you make an assessment about the other person is core to how you actually trust them.

I'll introduce you at a deeper level than has been the case to date to the notions of 'the legitimate other' and 'legitimate self', and how that is so important to how we give trust to others. That is, if trust is ever a gift, rather than an outcome. I'll also share with you the latter stages of the commitment cycle, which relate to the other person and how it comes back to the two of you when making requests and offers. I'll share the intersection and the model between trusting others and your Way of Being, which leads to the importance of trust in building relationships. I'll also go into the heart of the model, which is you delivering on your commitments.

Trust and 'the Legitimate other' and 'Legitimate self'

The idea of 'the legitimate other', which is an ontological term, is to hold the person you are in a relationship with, conversation with, meeting with or simply in the presence of as legitimate.

Alan Sieler, in *Coaching to the Human Soul volume one*, describes 'the legitimate other' as, "A person of equal validity, not better and not worse." They are legitimate human beings. Linked to that, they believe their views are legitimate based on their cultural beliefs, their family experience, and their lived experience [referring to the 'stories' Venn diagram in chapter one]. You don't have to agree with them or even like them. However, they believe that what they're saying has legitimacy and that they're legitimate human beings. You should do the same. This, for me, is at the heart of being able to lead a diverse team effectively.

"If you can allow yourself to hold them as legitimate in the context of their humanness and their stories, ask questions for clarity or even support them in grounding what they're saying, you will have a more fruitful conversation and/or relationship with them.

More than that, you will start to trust them as you understand better where they're coming from [their Way of Being]. In an existential way, you can also be 'the legitimate other' to them. To yourself, you are 'the legitimate self'" – Alan Sieler, in *Coaching to the Human Soul volume one*.

Holding both the other person and yourself as legitimate is fundamental to you trusting that person because you will hold them as equal. You won't allow your stories, standards, assessments, judgments, and beliefs to get in the way of you hearing theirs. It will also help you be present in the company of the other person. To do this effectively, you have to be a learner and be in a mood of curiosity.

Think how many times you're not present when someone is talking to you. You're absent-minded or you're thinking of your own concerns. By doing this, you are not holding the person as 'the legitimate other', you are not being curious and you are certainly not being a learner.

By holding yourself as the 'legitimate self', you're not allowing yourself to be tied to the assessment others make of you. You are true to your own assessments, stories, feelings, and beliefs – all of which will stand you in good stead for legitimising others. You may like to imagine a spectrum of to the left 'not holding yourself as legitimate' and to the right you 'holding yourself as fully legitimate'. As you read this now, where are you on this spectrum? Do you feel you may be 'outsourcing your self-legitimacy'? What can you do to shift the pointer further to the right, to serve you better? In my coaching and mentoring I find that there is a causal link between 'the legitimate self' with both 'self-esteem' and 'self-confidence' (as well as executive presence). What follows may support you exploring these aspects more deeply in yourself.

I was part of an amazing conversation of discovery on this topic recently with leaders in industry, who happened to all be women. Why was this so? It was part of the mentoring that I am privileged to 'do', in the domain of women in leadership with NAWO (*www.nawo.org.au*).

During our conversation one of the leaders introduced the distinction between self-confidence and self-esteem, and it would be fair to say that all of us had differing views on the distinction – which was the beauty of the conversation.

For one, self-confidence was more a variable depending on the situation, and self-esteem more of a constant; for another, self-confidence was more about a competency in the moment and self-esteem more about the inner self; for another, self-esteem was the driver of self-confidence, and for me, initially I felt self-confidence was more related to the inner self (our way of being) and self-esteem was more about how others might perceive you based on your behaviour and how you take action (in your way of doing).

What did we do with our different interpretations? We went to Dictionary.com to be learners and to educate ourselves! We found this:

Self-confidence – *realistic confidence in one's own judgment, ability, power, etc.*

Self-esteem – *a realistic respect for or favourable impression of oneself; self-respect.*

It was at this point in the conversation that I introduced the group to the notion of 'the legitimate self', which I felt was more aligned to the distinction of self-esteem, rather than self-confidence.

Following this session we collectively wrote a paper on this topic that was shared on LinkedIn in April 2022. In a comment on that post I was asked by a coaching colleague, Katherine Riddoch: "Is it a bit like the chicken and the egg? Can they be independent or are they co-dependent?"

This is such a great question and I want to address it here. As I share above, if you choose to learn something where your self-confidence may be low and you improve or even master it, then there is a fair chance that in some way your self-esteem will be impacted in a way that serves you well. Why? Because the stories you tell yourself about this particular skill will be self-affirming, and as those self-narratives (your stories) are core to your 'way of being', it will probably help build your self-esteem.

However, if your 'way of being' is 'below the line' and you are in a mood of, say, resentment or resignation or anxiety, then even if your self-confidence in a particular aspect of doing improves, your self-esteem will be more affected by your mood than by this improved skill.

Conversely, if you are in a mood of, say, curiosity or peace or ambition, then it is likely your self-esteem will be related to these moods that tend to serve you well, and as such your self-esteem too will be 'above the line'.

Is it possible to have low self-confidence and high self-esteem? Yes, I believe it is. Why? Because you can be low on confidence in a particular aspect of doing, however in all other aspects of your life you can be in a mood that serves you well (i.e. with high self-esteem). For me, as a relatively high handicap golfer, my self-confidence in executing a chip shot over a bunker to a fast-paced green and getting my ball to stay on the green is pretty low. Does that mean my self-esteem is unduly affected if I 'duff' my chip shot and it misses the green? No, it doesn't! Does it mean my self-confidence is lower if I have to try it again a few holes later? Yes, absolutely!

Is it possible to have high self-confidence and low self-esteem? Again, I believe it is. I can be confident in my ability to cook a great spaghetti bolognaise (something I reckon I am pretty competent at, and others say that is so). If aspects of my way of being are affecting my self-esteem at a particular time and I am feeling low, can I still be self-confident to cook a good 'spag bol'? Yes. However, it is fair to say that if someone were to criticise that meal and my self-esteem was low, that criticism could 'take it lower'.

Is there a relationship between the two? Yes. Are they co-dependent? No.

In a separate coaching session to this mentoring session, I was working with a client in the domain of 'executive presence' and we referred to this distinction. We discussed how either, or both, of these notions were part of having or not having 'executive presence'. We concluded that having 'presence' has an equal level of both self-confidence and self-esteem – as well as how a person 'carries themself' in their body and physiological posture.

So, what are the key takeaways here related to 'the legitimate self'?

- The distinction that self-confidence is more to do with your ability (your 'way of doing') and self-esteem is more to do with your inner self (your 'way of being'). By observing which domain you are assessing, you can take different actions to remedy either, or both.

- The link of self-confidence to a standard that you set for yourself or hold yourself to, that might not be warranted in a particular situation.

- That the feeling of imposter syndrome can be looked at in terms of self-confidence in the domain of both competency and self-esteem. It is helpful to ask yourself in which domain is the imposter syndrome surfacing?

- That a lack of self-confidence can be overcome by choosing to be a learner and taking action in the domain of learning both more technical and transferable skills, which will enable you to take action to a higher standard in a particular domain.

- That there is a clear link between the legitimate self and executive presence, in so much as both self-esteem and self-confidence are core to 'having presence'.

- That all of these distinctions are related to how you do, or don't, trust yourself in your way of being.

Going back to 'the legitimate other', Chris Chittenden, a leading Australian ontological professional, puts it like this in his paper, 'The Legitimate Other': "We can most effectively engage with others if we hold that the way they observe and act in the world is legitimate for them. We term this holding them as the legitimate

TRUST

other. Everyone is a different observer of the world and each one of us is always interacting with people who have different interpretations of the world to what we hold. Sometimes these interpretations are markedly different from ours and this can create a significant challenge for us in dealing with others at times. This can be particularly valid if we find ourselves in a work or personal relationship that is ongoing."

Let's put this into practice and test the theory. I'm not proud to share with you that, when using this distinction as I was growing up, I didn't hold those in the arts with the same legitimacy as those in the sports arena. Why is that? For as long as I can remember, arts and acting were just not for me. I was a sports lad, and that did not go hand in hand with the stage. I also grew up with the story my father told me about his younger brother 'giving away his wicket' at school while playing cricket, so he could go and act in the school play that afternoon. To my father, this was 'just not cricket'. I'm not sure he's ever forgiven his brother to this day!

It was not until my children started acting on the stage that I really started to appreciate (legitimise) the act of acting by watching them in school plays. In the case of our son, he was part of an amateur dramatic company when he was a child and that is when I really started to appreciate the importance of acting on their personal development. Ironically, I now find myself on the advisory board of a theatre company, the Antipodes Theatre Company in Melbourne, where the standard of acting and the talent of those involved is quite incredible.

By not legitimising those in that sector, it affected my ability to trust their Way of Being and their Way of Doing. I would say, "Why would anyone want to be on stage?" This is close-minded, based on my biases and stories, not open-minded, not being curious, not

156

being a learner and not listening to their stories, their beliefs and experiences that led them to be on stage. How often do you do this without knowing it? Without getting too heavily into the politics of the era in which I write this book, when #BlackLivesMatter is at the fore, I ask myself now, how open have I been to the systemic shortfalls that have affected Black people and their ability to play an equal part in our society? The leading voices of this movement say that this is the challenge they have faced forever and face to this day. Have I seen their plight as 'the legitimate other'? I'm not sure I have – based on my cultural narrative, my family upbringing, and my own lived experience. This is not to criticise my upbringing, but to say that I'm now more open to learning in this space every day to rectify that. How do I do this? By listening to their stories and lived experiences and, as such, legitimising them and their narrative more than I've ever done.

In a different domain of 'the legitimate other' is diversity and inclusion within both your team and society. How you see, and take action, this topic is so critical to your leadership today.

"All teams are diverse". If that is so, it rests on what you determine as "diverse" within a team.

In a mentoring group I recently facilitated, we believed it could be:

- Diversity of gender
- Diversity of sexual preferences
- Diversity of age
- Diversity of culture and ethnicity
- Diversity of thought
- Diversity in how people learn
- Diversity of life experience
- Diversity of political beliefs

- Diversity of what one has never done before – i.e. diversity of one's 'comfort zone' to another's
- Diversity of what standards we accept
- Diversity of time zones in a global team
- Diversity of how the working week/contract is structured – full time/part time/contract/permanent etc.

We concluded there are more, however from a leadership perspective our conclusion was – don't see diversity only in the realm of the top four above – it is so much more. Culture and race (and therefore diversity) are not always visible or audible.

As a leader by opening yourself up to this possibility, it will enable you to be a more effective leader of your team that is probably more diverse than you ever realised it to be.

As diversity is not always visual and explicit you have to look and listen for it. This is at the heart of the notion of 'the legitimate other'.

So, if teams are more diverse than you believed them to be, how do you lead them effectively? We discussed this in the second part of our session, and I hope that what we concluded supports you consider how to be a more effective leader of a diverse team:

- Become a better listener to hear where the people in your team 'are coming from'. What is their story? What are their beliefs, and life experiences, that you can hear and have empathy with?
- Believe that your team is constantly developing its diversity through people's life experiences – it is not static.
- Observe your own 'way of being' – what stories are you telling yourself about diversity and what it is/is not? Acknowledge and question your own biases. What are you

feeling in your energy when you see diversity? What is your body telling you about this topic?

- Adapt your style accordingly to embrace the power in the diversity – which is ever changing.
- Acknowledge that times are changing, and as such, so is what diversity is within these changing times – e.g. Covid-19/current inflation/wars
- Observe how your team engages with each other – what role does diversity have in this?
- Understand the broader culture around you and where your team is operating – for example say, in a First Nations culture in FNQ/NT or far north WA.
- Build relationships – to at least a point of understanding the diversity. Do your research (however don't be blinded by your own biases) and have conversations for understanding. These conversations may be courageous and hard – however, have them.
- Acknowledge time zones if you are leading internationally and what are the associated cultural norms on this domain.
- When you recruit – be aware of diversity and build it into your recruitment process.

Most important of all be a learner and open to learning – without this you will not be an effective leader of a diverse team. Indeed, if you are not a learner, you probably won't recognise that you are leading a diverse team!

In an Orwellian conclusion:

> *"All teams are diverse, however some teams are more diverse than others."*

NAWO Mentoring Circle LinkedIn Paper June 2022

Practical application

In my work leading a Global Coaching Initiative we initially posted a LinkedIn banner of a white hand holding the globe. At first glance, because of my stories and lens on life, this looked great as we wanted to show that our aim was to change the course of global wellbeing, and it was the supportive hand of our vision that was doing this. However, it was pointed out to me by one of the coaches in the group, who was much more aware and in tune than I in this space, that this could be seen as a symbol of white patronage, and not in keeping with what #BlackLivesMatter is talking about systemic racism. You may think this is taking it too far. I acknowledge and accept that, however, I now don't see it that way. By listening and holding true to 'the legitimate other' and this person's stories and experience, it did make me reflect, and we decided to change the banner based on this conversation. Core to making this decision was being curious, being a learner as well as finding courage and being vulnerable. For me this action related directly to being vulnerable to the actions of 'the legitimate other' – in this case, my colleague in CoachAid. I would like to thank my colleague for this new learning. It created a new reality for me. As I shared before, 'a conversation creates a new reality'.

Another example of 'the legitimate other', that I'm sure you can relate to is your mobile phone. How often do you look at your mobile phone when you're at the dinner table, in a meeting or watching television with someone? In all of these instances, are you choosing to look at your phone as opposed to engaging in the conversation? You are not holding that person as a legitimate other. You're not present for them and you are choosing yourself over them. We do this all the time.

You don't have to trust everyone simply because you legitimise them. By holding the person as the legitimate other, hearing their stories and assessing why they are saying what they are saying or doing, you may come to the belief or have the feeling that you just don't want to trust them. That is fine. Just because you legitimise someone's humanness and their stories doesn't mean you have to trust them. However, if you don't legitimise their humanness and their stories, then it's virtually impossible to trust them.

If someone's a convicted criminal for a crime that you don't want to attempt to legitimise, that is understandable. However, you may be one of those professionals where legitimising the other to defend them in the legal system is critical to their defence or rehabilitation.

'The Legitimate Other' and listening

Such an important aspect of 'the legitimate other' is listening, and how you listen. Consciously listen to where the other person is coming from. What is their cultural story? What is their family story? What is their lived experience? Open yourself up to listening to this without listening to your biases and closing yourself off from hearing them. In my Coaching Practice, I call this 'talking to the other person's listening'. Think of 'person three' and 'person four' in my model of 'four people in a conversation'. Are you asking questions and being curious to hear their inner voice (their listening) to ensure that you are on the same page? Are you leaving 'space' between listening and talking?

Practical application

Ask yourself, when you're in the presence of anyone or in a conversation with someone, if you are holding them as 'the legitimate other'. If for any reason you feel you're not, then listen to them consciously. As ontologist Chyonne Kreltszheim put it so wonderfully in a post on LinkedIn in 2020, "Conscious listening isn't something you do, it's a Way of Being. And it's based on four key qualities – presence, acceptance, compassion, tenacity." You may note that I've used the term 'conscious listening' throughout this book, rather than 'active listening'. Thank you, Chyonne.

Think about the relationship between presence, acceptance, and especially compassion, when you're trying to hold a person as 'the legitimate other'. As for tenacity, be tenacious in doing it. Once you hold the person as 'the legitimate other', you can make the choice to start trusting them or not.

You may have come across the term 'whole body listening' that is taught in primary schools today? Children are being taught to employ 'whole body listening', a term introduced in a publication of the American Speech-Language-Hearing Association (ASHA) in 1990, by Susanne Marie Poulette (Truesdale), MS in Ed, CCC-SLP. A visual use of this is depicted in my LinkedIn post on this subject in September 2020, where children are asked to consider how they listen with their eyes, ears, mouth, hands, feet, body, brain, and heart. It is so aligned to the notion of both Way of Being and Way of Doing. You might want to consider using this technique yourself – it is not only applicable to children. I wish I had been taught this depth of listening in my primary school years, not just being told to 'shut up and listen'!

Finally, in the space of listening, why not try **WAIT**? It stands for "Why am I talking?" If you can't answer that question, don't talk, listen!

The barriers to doing this are immense; I accept that. Firstly, you have to listen to your own biases and recognise them. This has been covered in previous chapters around understanding your Way of Being and your Way of Doing, through the stories you live in and those that live in you as well as how you take action. Then you need to consciously listen to the other person and hold them as 'the legitimate other', regardless of any trappings or societal labels you may place on them. Hear them and legitimise them as humans, that does not necessarily mean you have to trust them. As Chris Chittenden says, "Hold that the way they observe and act in the world is legitimate for them." Only then will you know if the person is someone you want to place your trust in and build a relationship with. This is also fundamental to leading a diverse team effectively.

This is the intersection in my model between Way of Doing and trusting others.

Trust and The Commitment Cycle – stages two, three and four

I'll now provide you with stages two, three and four of the commitment cycle, that I referred to in chapter five. The model will enable you to coordinate action, lead more effectively and build better relationships by using language more effectively.

Understanding the commitment cycle in its entirety gives you a framework to getting commitment for your request or offer. It also gives you the opportunity to be more open to others – listening to how they make meaning of what you ask them to do or what you offer to do for them. By having this distinction, you'll have the clarity of meaning in what you request and how you hear the response. You'll be more open to possibilities and cut out waste in your organisation by coordinating action more effectively.

If you don't understand that people have options when a request is made of them, and you don't make the feedback loop clear, then time is wasted, standards are not delivered on, relationships are damaged and, trust is either not created or trust that has been created erodes.

The commitment cycle

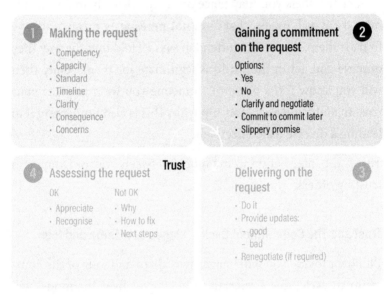

When we make a request of someone, they have five options. This is phase two of the cycle – 'gaining a commitment on the request'. Their options are:

1. **Yes.**

2. **No.**

3. They ask for **clarity** and **possible negotiation** on the deadline or standard. In this response, they will be assessing their capacity and competency – either knowingly or not. Be aware of this. They might therefore say, "I am too busy" as a reason to negotiate. Think about what they are really saying, when they say this – what could it actually be and what is 'hidden' in their language?

Could it be:

- I don't know/I need help with my priorities.
- I don't have the capacity to do what I need to do.
- I have concerns that need taking care of that may be outside of work and as such are 'making me busy'.
- I don't have the competency to do this, but I can't say it to you, or even myself.

If you hear the word 'busy' in this context, what ultimately are your options? How can you make an offer to help them 'get out of' the busyness?

4. They **'commit to commit later'** – they say they will give a response to the request; however, they will not give a response until a particular time. If you hear this response, get a time from them where they will make the commitment to give you a response. The later response could still be a no or a negotiation. If they miss this agreed time, then they have failed on a commitment and trust is either broken or starts to erode. The person may hear this as a no – if this is the case try again to 'talk to their listening' (voice 4) that this is not a 'no', but a commitment to respond later.

5. They give us a **'slippery promise'**. "She'll be right, mate," or, "Yep, no worries," as some Aussies might say, or "Yeah, I got that covered," or, "All good," or, "Leave it with me." You get the drift. If you accept a 'slippery promise', then you are at fault. *Never* accept a 'slippery promise' in a leadership position. However, if you are a parent, you'll know that children are best at giving parents slippery promises and it's difficult not to accept them!

The commitment cycle

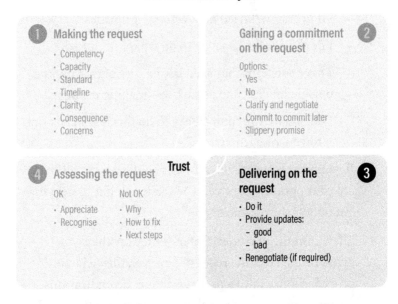

Phase three of the cycle is the person delivering on the request. If you like metaphors, I see this as the person running as fast as they can down the back straight in a 4x100m relay, holding that baton tightly, which is your request in their hand. The bond of trust between you and that person will be cemented by how they deliver on their commitment. They have three responsibilities in the bond of trust that's being created in phase three:

1. They do it and they tell you when it's done.

2. Provide updates. It is their responsibility to provide you with updates, both good and bad. Make sure that is the standard that you uphold. This also will ensure that you're not seen as the micromanager if that is your style.

3. If they can't do it, either to a time or a standard, they have to make sure that they let you know in a timely fashion and potentially renegotiate.

Potentially core to them taking this element of the cycle seriously is not only the value they place on delivering on their commitment, but also having clarity on the consequence of not delivering. As you know, this is a critical element of phase one of the cycle – making that consequence clear.

The commitment cycle

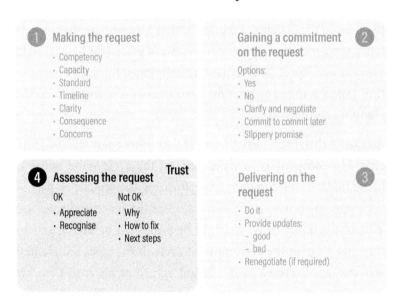

1 Making the request
- Competency
- Capacity
- Standard
- Timeline
- Clarity
- Consequence
- Concerns

2 Gaining a commitment on the request
Options:
- Yes
- No
- Clarify and negotiate
- Commit to commit later
- Slippery promise

4 Assessing the request — Trust

OK	Not OK
· Appreciate	· Why
· Recognise	· How to fix
	· Next steps

3 Delivering on the request
- Do it
- Provide updates:
  - good
  - bad
- Renegotiate (if required)

Phase four of the cycle is the assessment of their making good on their commitments, which is where the assessment of trust is ultimately made. Has it been done well? If so, have a conversation for appreciation or recognition. Has it not been done well to a time or standard? If not, have a conversation for performance or clarity of expectations. At this stage, think about forgiveness and your Way of Being, and how you may or may not wish to forgive them for not delivering to the standard or time.

Let's have a look at a story using this framework. I've recently made a request of a builder. I'm satisfied that the request made has been understood as we had a conversation for clarity, and I gained a commitment to both a date and a standard. The context of this request is that a new house is being built behind our house and it materially changes the aspect of our backyard. A double-storey townhouse will be overlooking our fence where previously there was an old single-storey house that we could see straight over to the trees in the distance. I requested that his company erect a new fence at their cost and plant new trees at a particular height, all to support our aspect. This request actually came through a negotiation from his initial request for us to remove our objection to the planning commission!

As I write this, I still have the belief that my request will be delivered. His company is in stage three of the cycle – the house is being built, so his company is performing the request as part of the cycle, in so much as the erection of the fence and trees are 'part of the build'. This book will be published before he gets to the final stage of the commitment cycle. If the trees are planted and the fence erected to the height agreed at his cost, then his commitment has been delivered and trust will be built. However, if neither of those are delivered, then the trust I placed in the builder will be eroded, if not completely gone – depending on our follow-up conversation, no doubt.

The purpose of sharing this story is that the model is applicable in all realms of life, not only professionally and in the leadership domain of making requests.

Now let us look at this in the realm of offers. Again, the recipient of your offer has the same five choices around whether to accept your offer of service/support or not. When you are delivering on the offer, you are in stage three of the commitment cycle. You are delivering on your own offer, so it is incumbent on you to keep the person you have made the offer to informed, and ultimately to deliver on your commitment of the offer made. Should you do so, trust is built. If it is not delivered, trust will then be diminished.

Using the commitment cycle every time you make a request or offer seems like a lot of work. Yes, it is. However, by putting in the planning up front and taking the time to make an effective request or offer by ensuring in stage two that you won't receive a slippery promise, you will save time. Think of the six Ps saying, shared in chapter five.

By assigning the other person the responsibility to provide you with feedback to an agreed standard at agreed times to you, then you will save time and effort. This is an integral aspect of Covey's assessment of trust.

I'm not sure there are exceptions to this model, to be honest. You can tone down the use of language. Instead of making it absolutely clear, "I am making a request," you might say, "I have something to ask you to do." However, in any circumstance, making a clear request (or instruction), gaining unambiguous commitment to the time and standard expected, and ensuring the person takes responsibility for giving feedback while doing the task, is basic to getting the job done well and builds trust.

One exception I can think of in the realm of stage three (the feedback loop), is where an ex-sales director colleague of mine in the UK, Nigel Jew, once shared with me, "Conor, you get what you inspect, not what you expect." I advise you, as a leader, to still do some inspecting in stage three, although not so much that you'll seem to be micromanaging. To ensure you are not micro-managing, ask yourself this question: "Am I leading at the right level?" Think too of the statement popularised by Ronald Reagan, "trust but verify". However, don't 'dip down' as Martin G. Moore calls it in his book *No Bulls!t Leadership*, where he provides two distinctions between 'dipping down' and 'inspecting progress': "The first is the level of detail interrogated. Having regular checkpoints to satisfy yourself that a particular piece of work is on track is essential – as long as it doesn't become an inquisition into every minute detail. The second difference is how you articulate the enquiry. When things go off track, the role of the good leader is to ask good questions focused on the agreed outcomes to understand why the problem has occurred, and what needs to be done to get it on track." Finally, in this domain of 'inspecting and expecting', I ask you to ask yourself, "am I being curious when I inspect, or am I looking for issues to prove me right?" Clearly being curious is the way to go here! It's a difficult balance, for sure.

Practical application

Listen the next time you hear a response to a request or offer that you make. Do you hear and accept a slippery promise? If you do, then go back to the person and get a commitment from them. Are you sure the person has clarity on your request, including the time, standard and consequence? If not, go and clarify. Have you asked about their concerns regarding your request? Have you made it clear that it's their responsibility to feed that progress to you, not your responsibility to go chasing them? If not, go and make that expectation clear. Have you had the conversation for performance if they've not delivered on the request to your agreed time and standard? If not, go and have the conversation for performance. Have you had the conversation for appreciation and/or recognition if they have delivered to the time and standard? If not, go and have the conversation for appreciation and recognition, which is in Stage Four of the cycle.

It's a choice whether to use this model or not. If you choose not to use it, ask yourself, "What am I doing instead to ensure my requests and offers are clear, so that I gain a commitment from the person I'm making the request of, where they give me feedback on their progress and I either say thank you or make their shortfall in the performance clear?" If you can't answer those questions, and you're not getting the traction or results you want from those who work for you, then why not give this approach a try? What have you got to lose?

Trust and relationships

This is the intersection between trusting others and your Way of Being.

As stated in chapter three, 'building relationships is an outcome of legitimising the other and self, taking care of the other person's concerns, and communicating effectively'.

It is at the heart of the 'V, I and S' of the Seven Assessments of Trust – are you vulnerable and open to being vulnerable to the other persons' actions, are you invested in the relationship as well as that person's concerns and are you sincere in that assessment?

Rob Cross, in his 2019 *Harvard Business Review* article 'To Be Happier at Work, Invest More in Your Relationships' states, "The importance of relationships is backed up by research. Studies show that social connections play a central role in fostering a sense of purpose and well-being in the workplace. They also impact the bottom line: Effective management of social capital within an organisation facilitates learning and knowledge sharing, increases employee retention and engagement, reduces burnout, sparks innovation, and improves employee organizational performance."

I don't think that I can put it any more succinctly than that. If you don't focus on your relationships in your place of work, then a number of key success factors in your performance will be affected. That will lead to a loss of trust in you and, as we've established, your brand and reputation will be tarnished.

The word "connections" in Cross's article leads into another core aspect of the importance of relationships, which is your mental health and that of your team. As Genevieve Hawkins, author of *Mentally at Work*, shares: "If you cannot master how to connect with others, not only will your career suffer, but your mental health will too". Connection is at the heart of building relationships, and relationships are key to creating and building trust.

In regard to building relationships and trusting others as a leader, it's important to be able to delegate effectively and hold others accountable. As Jesse Sostrin wrote in the 2017 *Harvard Business Review* article 'To Be a Great Leader, You Have to Learn How to Delegate Well', "Elevating your impact requires you to embrace an unavoidable leadership paradox: you need to be more essential and less involved." I've taken this to mean delegation, which I covered in more detail in chapter two.

The 2016 World Economic Forum executive summary report on future skills in the workplace states that, "On average, by 2020, more than a third of the desired core skillsets of most occupations will be comprised of skills that are not yet considered crucial to the job today, according to the respondents. Overall social skills, such as – persuasion, emotional intelligence, and teaching others – will be in higher demand across industries than narrow technical skills, such as programming or equipment operation and control. In essence, technical skills will need to be supplemented with strong social and collaboration skills."

Today we see that social skills are imperative to relationship building – all of which are part of both our Way of Being and our Way of Doing. In my model, I'm drawing the relationship link between you trusting your Way of Being and holding the other person in the relationship as legitimate, which is linked to your Way of Doing. The commitment cycle, using a technique in language, is a part of this. However, core to building effective relationships at work are making connections, knowing both your Way of Being and your Way of Doing, and holding the other as 'the legitimate other'.

As you know, without trusting others, you will not be able to delegate, which we have covered previously. Without effectively delegating, you will not be a successful business leader or have strong working relations, be you a CEO, business owner, head-teacher, C-Level leader, or next-gen executive leader.

I make the link in my model between circle three and circle one as building relationships, because it is an outcome of a process. It is the outcome of the process of the inner rings in my model and New Ordering of Trust – observing your Way of Being, observing your Way of Doing, and trusting others – that leads right back to your Way of Being.

Where I feel my working relationships were at their best was at National Foods between 2006 and 2010, when I was in flow. I didn't label it as that at the time, however I re-narrate my story to seeing it as that now. My working relationships with my boss, my peers, those who worked for me and those I influenced as an executive leader were strong. I felt this through the types of conversations I had with those individuals and the results we collectively achieved relative to the targets and objectives that we set.

When I look back using my model and New Ordering of Trust and review it against whether I trusted others and they trusted me, there is complete alignment between the strong relationships, the results we delivered and my Way of Being and Doing. The evidence of this is a framed picture of our values in that organisation, which hangs on the wall as I write this book for you, covered with appreciative notes from those I worked with – "Thanks for your friendship and support. We certainly made a few things happen," from a peer; "Conor, passion, commitment, perseverance, integrity are what comes to mind! You have certainly made your mark on me personally as well as NF," from another peer; "Conor, you have left your world in better shape than when you started. A fair legacy," from a direct report; "Thanks for your leadership, counsel, and challenge. Destination zero is something that we can be mightily proud of. It has changed National Foods and its people," from a direct report.

The importance of good relationships, trusting others, and being trusted by others is key to having an enjoyable time at work and delivering results, all of which are a core part of my model and New Ordering of Trust.

Another area in which relationships and relationship building are crucial is in the management of your career. How you build relationships – network – is indispensable to you being able to solve other people's problems which, if you think about it, is all you really need to do throughout your career to create value, based on your labour. The output of solving those problems is that it takes care of your concern of having a career that works for you. If you go about it the other way – your career is about solving your problem of personal career development – it will catch you out. I can attest to that.

When you are considering moving roles or your role has been retrenched for some reason, flip the notion that you are looking for your next role for you. You are looking for your next role for someone else. I say to my clients who are in this position, "You are an offer to solve someone else's problem. Your role in this stage of your career is to find the problem that you can solve." It's your responsibility to know what problem you are able to, and want to, solve in the reflection stage of career transition. However, to keep this relative to relationship building and the building of trust in this space of career transition, you need to have 'conversations for relationships' initially, otherwise known as networking. Following this conversation, you may have 'conversations for possibilities and opportunities', but this in *not* where you start. You may want to revisit the 'types of conversations' we covered in the last chapter to understand what a 'conversation for relationships' is and what the KPI is that leads from it. Key to this transition is seeking advice, not asking for a job. A leading career transition coach and author of *Building a Winning Career*, William Cowan AM, shared this with me in 2010 when he was my career coach after leaving National Foods: "If you ask for a job, you will get advice. However, if you ask for advice, you will get a job." The context here is that when you know what it is you are looking for and you know what problems you are trying to solve, you can get out there and find the problems that you can solve. You do this by building relationships and asking for advice as part of your research. It is through this process that people will trust that you are able to solve either their or someone in their network's problem. From there, you will find your next role and you will start the role with trust created. You are the solution to someone else's problem because you have taken the time and effort to build a series of relationships which hopefully will be there for the rest of your career. I also share with my clients in this space that those you network with in the marketplace, 'will help you find what you are looking for, they won't help you work out what you are looking for'. So please, if you are in career transition and looking to build relationships through networking, know what problems you want to solve (i.e. work out what you are looking for), before you actively network and build new relationships.

By the way, I also strongly advise you to continue to build relationships or your network even when you are not looking for a role.

#FTSOW, you might say. Because it will help build your brand as a problem solver and someone who can be trusted.

You might say, "Isn't networking selling yourself?" It's not. It's about building relationships and finding problems that you might be able to solve. This includes sharing respectfully your network, because you might personally not be able to solve the person's problem. However, you know someone in your network who might be able to, and that builds trust.

You may say, I can get things done without everyone having to like me and without them having to trust me in their life. That's true. However, I'm not talking about everyone liking you. That's not my benchmark of having good relationships at work. If they like you, great. But they don't have to like you. They need to respect you as a person for the competency with which you lead, your demonstrated behaviour and, that they assess you as being vulnerable, which includes to their actions as well as how you take care of their concerns. That is my benchmark of a good relationship as a leader. Trusting you with their life is also not the benchmark I'm referring to. Are you holding each other as 'the legitimate other'?

Are you both delivering on your commitments to each other every day? These are the KPIs of trust in a workspace and in life.

Practical application

How are your working relationships? How do you know? How are you trusting of others and how do people trust you? If you're not able to answer all or any of these questions, take some time to reflect on these questions:

1. #FTSOW do I feel I need to have effective working relations?
2. #FTSOW do I need to build trust and be trusted by others?
3. Do I have effective working relations? How can I ground this assessment?
4. Do I trust those I work with, for, and who work for me? Do they trust me? How can I ground the assessments I come to?

To ground these assessments, *ask*. Have some 'conversations for working relations'. We'll cover this in more detail in the next chapter, when talking about trust within teams.

The barriers to understanding how strong your relationships are is understanding that you are making an assessment of trust both ways. The way to address this is a personal reflection and then conversations with those who, after your reflection, you feel you want to explore your relationships and level of trust with. This is not easy and will probably require courage and curiosity – both attributes to being in an above the line mood, using the moods framework in chapter three.

Tim Ford, CEO of Treasury Wine Estates, a Global Wine Company, whose company ambition is "to be the most admired premium wine company in the world", does an exercise every day on his way home, in this domain, that you may find useful. In his own words, on 'No Limitations' podcast with Greg Robinson, "I have a process that I go through every day. I assess how I have performed that day – every interaction I have had, every meeting I have had. It's a 10-to-15-minute process I go through where I give myself a pass mark or not. It's a really important habit which I have been doing for the last seven or eight years now. It's more around the people interactions that I assess, than the business decisions. That often informs the call that I make on my way into work the next day!"

How much relationship building are you doing outside of your work? #FTSOW I hear you say. To support others, solve their problems, build relationships, and build trust in you and your brand. Saying that networking is 'selling yourself' may be another barrier, but I hope I've scotched that premise above.

Trust and consistently delivering on your commitments

The centre of the model, the internal circle of trusting self, is delivering on your commitments. As I said on the opening page, I view trust as consistently delivering on your commitments to self and others. It only seems right and fair, therefore, that this is at the heart of my model of trust – DYCC.

Is trust given straight away? Or does it have to be earned? These are oft-asked questions regarding trust. It depends so much on each individual that there's no one answer to this. For some, they will give trust until it is broken. Perhaps they are the people who see the good in everything and everyone. In this case, a 'brick wall of trust' is complete when they first meet that person.

For others, they will only give trust when requests made are delivered or implied expectations of someone are never broken. For these people, the wall of trust is built brick by brick. It grows ever higher, depending on how someone delivers on their commitment or how they behave. The wall of trust can also be chipped away or smashed down, depending on the severity of the breach.

Ultimately, trust is being able to answer this question with an affirmative: *"Do I believe this person or thing will consistently deliver on its commitment to my expectations – either stated or not – with the intent of supporting me and taking care of my concerns?"*

If I say "Yes" to this question, and assess it against the Seven Assessments of Trust, then I am trusting of this person or thing. Clearly, a track record in delivery is necessary to the trust equation between you and that person – both ways.

If there's a breach in the delivery of the commitment, then trust will be eroded or broken, depending on the severity of the breach. However, it's possible to start the process of trust again if the brick wall is chipped or even smashed down, by asking the same question above and giving the person time to rebuild the wall through their actions. Finding acceptance or peace with a breach in trust is a prerequisite to shifting yourself above the line. Unless you can do this, then it will be exceedingly difficult or almost impossible to rebuild the brick wall of trust. You can revisit the moods framework in chapter four for how to shift your mood to peace, perhaps using Dethmer's '4 A's of Acceptance'.

Who do you trust most? Is it the person who has let you down and who broke a commitment made to you? I don't believe so. Given this, delivering on your commitment to self and others is at the heart of trust, and therefore the heart of my model and New Ordering of Trust.

Practical application

I'm not sure there's any exceptions to this. Simply ask yourself, if someone continues to fail to deliver on their commitment to you, will you trust them? Also, ask yourself, "Am I always delivering on my commitments to myself and to others?" Depending on your answer to this, how much do you trust yourself and how trustworthy are you?

Ask yourself, are you delivering on your commitment to the other person's expectation, either stated or not, with the intent of supporting that person and taking care of their concerns? If yes, you're trustworthy. And if not...

Conclusion

You've learned about 'the legitimate other' and 'legitimate self'. I've shared with you the three other stages of the commitment cycle and how, in both language and deed, this cycle is fundamental to you delivering on your commitments while holding others to account to deliver on theirs. The outcome is trust. You've learned about the importance of relationships and the topic of trust and effective leadership through the intersection between trusting others and your Way of Being. I've then taken you to the heart of the model, delivering on your commitments.

As with most of this book, it's about you looking inside yourself and asking the question, "How do you 'hold' others?" Are you legitimising them? Are you getting a commitment from them? Are you holding them to account on delivering on their commitment to you?

I hope you will now see everyone you meet as 'the legitimate other'. I hope you will gain a commitment from someone when you make a request, and you hold them to delivering on their commitment. I hope that you will focus on your relationships and ask yourself (and actually test, as Tim Ford does) how strong they really are. And I hope that you will always deliver on your commitment to self and others by ensuring that you are taking care of their concerns – and yours.

What's coming up?

In the final chapter, I will introduce you to the idea of Collective Trust, and how this thing keeps getting bigger and bigger. However, as you will see, it all ends back with you.

Seven

Collective Trust

CO'M model and Ordering of Trust

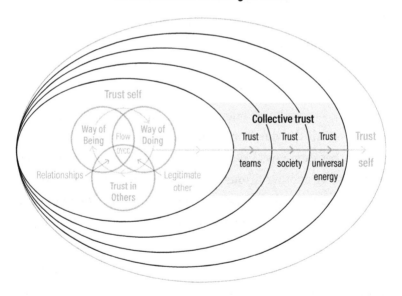

Trust is collective. It is bigger than you and bigger than your relationship with another person. It is also about your team, the society you live in and the 'universal energy' you are a part of. I call this Collective Trust.

In this larger domain of Collective Trust, there are four elements: a common purpose, a common intent, common standards, and common behaviours. I'll cover what these mean and apply them to the three concentric outer circles in my New Ordering of Trust model: team, society, and 'universal energy'.

Having looked at trust from within and trust with another, it's not possible to stop there. It has wider implications – hence the concentric circles in my model. How do you trust your team? How do you trust the society in which you live and in which you lead? Do you, and if so, how do you trust something that is much bigger than you and the world we all live in? Faith, spirituality, eastern philosophy, western religion, the cosmos, nature, the environment, it could even be in the domain of quantum physics that is the explanation for the relationship between atoms and particles – for me all of these fall under 'universal energy'. If I were not to address these areas, there's no wider context for you trusting yourself and trusting another.

Are the stories and methodologies that I've shared so far sufficient to answer all the questions you may have regarding trust and these other domains? I don't think so. I've covered trusting self and trusting another through my leadership stories, the models, and the examples that I've given you. I know that when I've gone deeper into the notion of trust without this wider context, it just doesn't feel complete.

I'll share the details of these four elements of Collective Trust with you, as well as the importance of Collective Trust with regards to your team. We'll talk about how to make a link to Collective Trust in society, and I will explore Collective Trust and the notion of 'universal energy' too. Finally, I will bring it all back to trusting yourself, as trust begins and ends with self.

Four common elements to Collective Trust

There are four common elements to Collective Trust when it comes to trusting more than yourself and trusting another. Without understanding these four elements, it's difficult to answer the question 'What is Collective Trust?' Based on my personal experience in life and as a leader in business, as well as the lessons I have gratefully learned from others, I believe the four areas of Collective Trust are: common purpose, common intent, common standards, and common behaviours.

Collective Trust Framework

Purpose

Intent

Collective
Trust

Behaviours

Standards

I, and a number of others are, as I write this book in 2020, creating a Global Coaching Initiative. I share this example as it is dear to my heart, and it shows you that I am putting my own model of Collective Trust into practice into a new creation. I write this in the present tense and will share with you later in the chapter how this has unfolded at the time of going to print.

Common purpose

Common purpose is the why and the what of your team, society, or belief. If you have this, it is likely that a Collective Trust will be created.

The initiative I refer to above was born from a desire to serve people through the initial challenges of Covid-19. On 30 March 2020, CoachAid20 attracted 350 Volunteer Coaches from every continent in less than a week. They – including myself as one of them – provided pro bono coaching sessions to every corner of the globe in just 10 days. The purpose of our new initiative is to promote "coaching interventions that change the course of global wellbeing". Our vision is "a global Not for Profit coaching service focused on supporting leaders of social change, and individuals impacted by rapid change and uncertainty". Our 'what' is "provide pro bono and affordable coaching around the globe".

As a team, we worked incredibly hard to create a shared purpose and vision from scratch when we all came together, not previously knowing one another at all. This was core to us building trust as a group of individuals who are now operating collectively as a team to launch this organisation. We have each other's backs.

In your context, please think of the purpose of your team/business. This will be directly related to your vision and mission. I do not get into the semantics here of the distinction between these two areas of business strategy. The core element of this top quadrant is alignment to something bigger than an objective or a number of priorities.

Common intent

Common intent is the how and for whom. The way that you collectively agree to coordinate action and carry out the task. Core to this is intent for others, not self. Sandra Sucher, Professor of Management at Harvard Business School, refers to this intent as "motives". She asks her students, and the readers of her book, to consider with regard to a company, "what are the motives beyond making money?" I love this line in her book *The Power of Trust*:

"we have to trust they have good intentions and do not intend to hurt us". This is an assessment we make of a company that is, in my view, aligned to the 'I' and the 'S' in the Assessments of Trust.

The question of intent and motive is also applicable to technology and systems, which are fundamental to how we all live our lives today. Those who create Artificial Intelligence (AI) and 'the internet of things' (IoT) must know their intent and motive for those who they create the system for. If you are the CEO of an organisation in this domain reading this, are you asking this question of yourself and your team/company?

If this permeates the outer circles of the model, collective trust will be built.

Returning to the Global Coaching Initiative as the example, our intent and 'how' is "supporting people in their challenges and opportunities; enabling growth through heightened self and systemic awareness; serving Not for Profit Organisations that focus on safety, food and shelter; aiding society through supporting their personal and professional needs." It is for others, not for us.

Common standards

Common standards are the clarity and agreement of standards in all domains, from seeing the possibility, to creating the opportunity to taking the action, to delivering the result. Without common standards, there will be no rule of law. Without a rule of law, it is near impossible – if not impossible – to create Collective Trust. With the Global Coaching Initiative, we are working on our common standards as I write this book. We are covering:

- the standards of coaches we invite to become members
- the standards of the services for the people we will coach

- the standards of the partners that we will work with and the standard of support that we will supply to them
- the standards of return we give to members and investors
- the standards of processes that facilitate how we operate
- the standards of leadership and Board governance that will ensure we serve the community we seek to serve and deliver on our vision and purpose.

In a recent Collective Trust engagement with a retailer here in Australia, the team I was working with agreed their collective standards to be:

- delivering on time
- communicating early and using the simplest of language
- emails having clarity in the headline and having clear expectations
- always leaving a meeting with clarity and action by asking 'by whom, by when and to what standard?'
- that the data provided to stakeholders will be evidence based and sources shared.

The final collective standard was, "I will always be present in a conversation and actively listen". As you can see from this example, 'Standards' as a word and as a notion should be seen as broad. Always remember your standards are an assessment, and they include your competency and capacity to deliver on them. In this domain, you are making the assessment regarding your team, society and universal energy.

Common behaviours

Common behaviours come from our values and are the visible delivery of the expectations of self and others. They are delivered predominantly when in the 'above the line set of moods' – as seen in the moods framework in chapter four. A visible set of behaviours that are common creates Collective Trust in that wider domain. Different teams and societies can have different behaviours, for sure. However, for Collective Trust to be built and created in that wider domain, having common behaviours is imperative. I have my colleague and friend in the Global Coaching Initiative, Scott McLaughlin, to thank here for challenging me on the notion of common values 'vs' common behaviours and which to openly share for an organisation – the beauty of behaviours, based on our values, is that they are a tangible demonstration by leaders, and all those in an organisation, that are visibly demonstrated through our 'Way of Doing', both in language and in deed.

With the Global Coaching Initiative, we have collectively agreed on three core behaviours: "care, clear, committed". Each of these has a clear meaning that we have outlined. Below each of these three words in our internal documentation are more detailed sets of behaviours that everyone involved in the initiative is buying into, and that others coming into it will incorporate into their Way of Being and demonstrate through their Way of Doing.

If you have all of these four common elements working in harmony, you will have Collective Trust. Let's test this thesis relating to team, society, and universal energy.

Do we all need to be in common to trust? Think about the idea of 'the legitimate other'. You don't have to be in common, or agree with or even like the other person, or team, or those in society. You don't have to believe what they believe in. However, you do have to legitimise them as a human and legitimise their story and their set of beliefs. You have to hold them as legitimate to trust them. If you find something in common in one or all four of these elements of collective trust, then it is highly likely that the collective trust in the outer circles will be created.

Where any one or all four of these elements are not present, we can see that collective trust is being eroded. Take the Covid-19 pandemic in 2020. With a different purpose/intent/standard and behaviour that's being exhibited by all global leaders, we have seen state against state in Australia in the second wave of the Melbourne lockdown, and country against country globally – leaving the World Health Organization (WHO), the global organisation whose role it is to create common trust, bereft of answers. There are no common purposes, intents, standards, or behaviours that I can see. Look at the US, Brazil and arguably the UK which took an 'open approach'. Sweden took a purposefully more liberal approach. New Zealand, Taiwan, Singapore, Uruguay, and Australia took a much more suppressive approach. There is nothing common here. In this current time at the back end of 2020, there is no worldwide Collective Trust in the approach to the Covid-19 global pandemic.

Practical application

Place these four areas of common trust against your team or business. Does your team have a common purpose? Does it have a common intent? Does it have common standards, and does it have common behaviours that are clearly exhibited by you and those in your team/business? Apply the same questions to the society you live in – however you determine society. Finally, apply these questions to what you believe in – if anything – from a perspective of 'universal energy', including western religion, eastern philosophy, nature or whatever you believe, or feel is a higher authority or energy.

As with many other areas of this book, the barrier you may face is you. Can you make the choice to observe these four elements in any of the Collective Trust circles that comes to you? If so, take action and do something about your observation if you feel that the collective trust in any one of the outer circles is not there. Create or recreate the common purpose, intent, standard and behaviour of your team, for example.

Collective trust in your team

Having looked at the four quadrants in the last section overall, let's apply it to your team and have a look at another example from my life.

Creating collective trust in your team is requisite to it delivering on its purpose and associated actions. Think of teams that you've been in that haven't delivered on their promise or purpose. What have been the common themes? Conversely, think of teams that have. Why have they succeeded?

A way of looking at Collective Trust in your team is "psychological safety." As Laura Delizonna wrote in her 2017 *Harvard Business Review* article 'Higher Performing Teams Need Psychological Safety', "The highest performing teams have one thing in common, psychological safety, the belief that you won't be punished when you make a mistake." She goes on to outline the five-step process that Paul Santagata, head of industry at Google, adopted. I will bring this notion of psychological safety into my story coming up.

The four quadrants in Collective Trust create this psychological safety and a feeling of belonging in the team. By having Collective Trust emanating from each of these four areas, it allows curiosity, openness to learn, diversity, inclusion and acceptance of challenging others to flourish.

I have shared with you earlier in the book that I was an executive on the leadership team at National Foods from 2006 to 2010. In December 2007, the leadership team decided to commit to buying Dairy Farmers, the major dairy competitor to National Foods at the time, that was openly up for sale. The executive team was split into two teams by the CEO – one to run the business, and the other to acquire Dairy Farmers. I will never forget that day prior to Christmas when, looking around the room at every person on each team, there was complete trust both that the CEO would divide the team correctly, and that each team trusted the other to do their collective job. Without a well-run business, there was no acquisition. Without an acquisition, the strategy of being the dominant dairy player in Australia, at that time, would not have come to pass.

If I look at each of these quadrants in relation to this, the purpose of the collective was clear, and the purpose of each team was clear. The purpose of the collective was to "be a leading branded food and beverage business in the Asia Pacific Region". By being the dominant dairy business in Australia we would have the scale to "perform and grow". This meant providing the best products and innovation in the sector to the consumers and customers, provide strong returns to our suppliers and shareholders, as well as possibly gaining some negotiating leverage with the retailers. The decision of Coles to sell house brand milk at $1 per litre to consumers a year later did severely challenge that strategy, in part at least!

The purpose of each team was to do their job to enable the other to do their job.

The intent of the group was that we would deliver for each other and our key stakeholders. The 'how' we delivered on that intent was by delivering on our commitment to ourselves and the others in the group.

The standard of the bid team was of the highest order and was key to us making the acquisition. The standard for the day job team was vital to us meeting customer and consumer needs and to grow the business.

We all, individually and collectively, lived the values that had been created after National Foods bought Berri in 2005 and which stood the test of time when we bought Dairy Farmers in 2008. Our values were: safety; teamwork; passion for success and our brands; respect for others; customer focus; innovation; integrity and social responsibility. Sitting underneath each of these values were specific behaviours that we created for all of us in the organisation to use as our 'how' in the action that we took.

It was announced on 25 August 2008 that National Foods had acquired Dairy Farmers. It was a team effort underpinned by a common purpose, common intent, common standards, and common behaviours – Collective Trust – and it was a privilege to have been part of it. In this example of Collective Trust there was definitely psychological safety in the team.

If you know this sector, it was argued at the time that National Foods/Kirin (the owner of National Foods) overpaid for Dairy Farmers. However, in that room in December 2007, there was complete Collective Trust and it continued through to the end of 2009 when National Foods merged with Lion Nathan and that team was broken up. In terms of price and strategy, hindsight is a wonderful thing!

Having collective trust, and trust in self and others, is needed for a team to deliver on its promise, so there is no exception. However, I do accept that at the time of writing, times are changing, and trust in teams is being redefined in the Covid-19 and post Covid-19 era, so I feel it is important to address that 'fact'.

How you are leading now and trusting your team is no doubt materially different to how it was previously, due to the increased numbers of people working at home. At the height of the Covid-19 pandemic, you may have been 'forced' to trust people working at home and it may have surprised you that in many cases, productivity increased – I see no surprise here re the link between trust and delivery of outcomes.

I was brought up and led in a time and environment where being seen in the office was core to our way of working. If you weren't seen, you weren't delivering. The outcome of this was too many hours worked, too many hours spent not delivering outcomes but 'being busy', and individuals being too scared to leave the office before the boss for fear of being thought of as lazy. Fortunately, those days have started to come to an end in certain industries, with the increased use of technology and working at home. However, in certain industries through the 2020 pandemic, that 'old school culture' was still pervasive. At the time of writing this has had repercussions for some of those leaders in those environments, when people chose not to follow them, as they took their labour elsewhere, to where they felt more trusted in the new technologically facilitated business environment.

An outcome of this is that trust in teams is being redefined. The redefinition of team trust simply sped up when the business community lived through the height of the Covid-19 pandemic. By using technology – both video technology and broader computing technology – you don't have to be present in the office to deliver on your promise. I do accept that in senior leadership roles, being seen and present is a core element to leading and building trust. However, in my view some leaders overplayed this in the Covid-19 pandemic and hid behind it as they went to the office every day. By doing this, if you did, did you set an example of what is possible as a leader, integrating working at home and working at the office, for others to follow?

The culture of having to be seen, so as not to be seen as lazy, is clearly a fallacy.

Two other reasons for this redefinition of trusting teams lies in two areas: humanism and language. In the Covid-19 pandemic you brought your professional and personal life visibly together. Your humanistic side of your working life was exposed through your Zoom, Microsoft Teams and Skype lenses, and your team was okay with it. You saw living rooms, kitchens, bedrooms, bikes, sewing machines, pets, partners, and children in the background – or even in the foreground in some cases – in meetings. In no way did it diminish the professionalism of what was being discussed.

This reliance on technology prompted the Poet Laureate in the UK (an honorary position appointed by the Monarch of the UK), Simon Armitage, to compose a poem on 1 October 2020, called *Something Clicked*. In stanza five (of six) he writes:[1]

> *It's a new world – you're at school in the kitchen,*
> *at work in the attic, in Ancient Rome in the lounge,*
> *on Mars in the basement. Why tear out your hair*
> *while the present dithers and loads, you deserve*
> *to lean on the airwaves and not fall over,*
> *to feel the hub of your heart's heart*
> *pulsating and purring with life's signal.*

---

1   Reproduced with permission.

In the press release accompanying the poem launch, BT (the Company sponsoring) and Armitage share that, "the one-off commission highlights the increased reliance on broadband in helping us stay connected in recent months. From keeping in touch with family and friends, to home schooling and taking up new hobbies, connectivity and broadband have never been so fundamental to so many parts of life." *(prsnewswire.co.uk)*

My take on this benefit is not only the connection that Armitage points out, but how technology can actually help you shift your mood to perform more effectively. If you are able to utilise the benefit of the screen and energy that connection can create, and be fully present, it may enable you to shift to a mood of curiosity or ambition which enables you to see possibilities, listen to others more intently and legitimise them as humans with a story to tell and a contribution to make. I am sure over time this technology will change, however on writing this book, the business world has taken years off plans it was making to use more technology effectively. It has enabled people who work at home to be both more productive and to integrate their life better between the work and home domains.

Linked to this humanistic world of bringing your professional and personal lives together through a lens are the increased check-ins and connectivity that you are initiating with your team – asking "Are you okay" far more than was ever done before, no doubt. By continuing to check in on your team's mental health and wellbeing, creating connection and by being inclusive, this feeling of psychological safety and belonging will grow. Trust in your team will be increased and the professional distancing of keeping home and work separate will continue to be eroded at a much quicker pace.

Another key factor in the changing dynamic of trust in teams through technology, is that you are more purposeful in your use of language to get stuff done in the age of working at home. You have to think about why you're calling for a meeting. Now you will be saying, "#FTSOW am I having this meeting or conversation?" As you know, it is imperative that, to coordinate action effectively as a leader, you are able to answer this question and also ask what your KPI of success is for this conversation or meeting. There isn't the opportunity to waste people's time by calling everyone into a huddle or a meaningless meeting just because they're in the office. That's not to say that all huddles and meetings are meaningless, but I'm sure you know what I mean.

The purposeful use of language makes for better conversations and the increased use of technology means this is more important. You will have a clear purpose and you will make better requests, because the opportunity of nipping back to someone's desk isn't there with fewer people in the office. With you being more humanistic as personal and professional lives come together, and by being more effective and purposeful with language, trust in teams is changing irrevocably, and for the better.

I'm not saying teams do not need to work in an office environment at all. The human need for human connection, and coming together personally is integral to the trust dynamic in the team, and this will be a core reason that people choose to go to the office, rather than 'to be seen'. The notion of trusting your team in the post Covid-19 era with better use of technology is here to stay. It builds trust by allowing people to deliver on their commitment without having to be seen as busy, and that is a positive thing.

Given this extra technological domain that we have now all become more proficient in conversing in, ask yourself which domain is best for me to have 'this' conversation?

I share with leaders I work with that you have three options here:

1. 'In person' (please do not label this as 'face to face').
2. 'Virtual face to face' – yes, I do see this as us conversing 'face to face', as we are able to see each other, get a read of the energy between us and make an assessment of each other's physiology, as well as the words and tone used.
3. On the phone. I find this can be best for the humanistic 'check in' call. You may even start to use your walking time to do this more often, so as to get away from your desk.

By asking yourself which domain to have your conversation in, you are adding to that conversation a deeper level of planning than purely #FTSOW and your KPI, as you are also bringing in a deep consideration of 'the legitimate other' by your choice of domain.

Practical application

To make an assessment of the trust in your team against each of the quadrants in the collective trust model, why don't you ask them? Show them the model, rate yourself, and then ask the team to rate the team on a scale of zero to 10 for each quadrant. See what emerges and with that information you can put a plan in place to move each quadrant up the scale towards 10.

You might also want to use my 'SES model', co-created with a client, by asking these three questions about your team relationship:

- How am I **seen** by the team? (your brand)
- What is the team's **experience** of working with me as the leader? (your Way of Doing)
- How can we **strengthen** our relationship as a team? (the trust in your team relationships)

(Built on the SET model, that you might be familiar with – 'seen', 'experience', 'talked about'.)

Ask yourself these questions too: "How am I trusting my team in the new working at home environment? How should I go about building trust in the new office environment when there is more working at home? What behaviours do I need to demonstrate to show what is possible with this new integration of working at home and working at the office?"

Have the courage to self-assess and the vulnerability to ask your team, and potentially other stakeholders who interface and rely on your team, these questions.

Collective trust and society

"Around the world, business innovation is leading to rapid and transformational changes in technology, consumption patterns and lifestyle aspirations. At the same time, societies are looking to businesses to lead change in response to urgent and systemic social and environmental challenges. These issues pose fundamental risks to the stability and wellbeing of societies, but also opportunities for adaptation. This changing context is driving dramatic shifts across whole sectors and economies, at a pace that requires not only new policy and governance frameworks, but also business responsibility and leadership." *Rewiring Leadership. The future we want, the leadership we need.* University of Cambridge, Institute for Sustainability Leadership, 2018.

Given the assessment above from a world-leading university, understanding the importance of your leadership role in society will facilitate you to lead these "systemic social and environmental challenges".

Trusting yourself and others, including your team, leads to how you trust the society you live in and lead in. Trusting the society you live your life in provides context for you trusting yourself, others, and your team. It grounds you and gives you an equilibrium, a sense of belonging, and an ability to plan for the future. Without this, your ability to lead in business is compromised. It is also critical to believe that not only do you lead your team and your business, you lead in society, as evidenced by the University of Cambridge quote above.

Having the role that you do, you directly influence society more than has ever been the case before. Technology, global reach of companies, internationalisation, the loss of trust in traditional institutions of state, church, and media, as well as the pace of change and global uncertainty have ensured that this is so.

In 2020 #MeToo, #BlackLivesMatter and the Covid-19 epidemic are challenging all of us and making us all question what we believe we know. Politically, pre 2020 the change in voting intent in America, the UK, India and Brazil and now in 2020 with the changes taking place in China and Hong Kong, we are questioning ourselves about what is happening in the society that we had become accustomed to in the post-cold war era.

As I shared on the *CoachAid20* website when we launched CoachAid20, in March 2020, "Society is living in a collective mood of anxiety in a world of uncertainty." We are questioning history. We are questioning standards. We are questioning what gender diversity, beyond the traditional binary lens of men and women, is. We are questioning the world order. In the year of writing this book, we are seeing industries like travel and hospitality being decimated. We are seeing changing work habits as millions work at home. We are seeing culture and businesses changing as the work environment changes. We are challenging what we collectively trust in this world of uncertainty, which is creating this collective mood of anxiety. These questions and movements are all part of your leadership challenge today, and if they are not, they should be.

The *Edelman Trust barometer*, which has surveyed trust and credibility around the world for the last 20 years and is trusted globally, wrote in January 2020 (before the Covid-19 pandemic) "that despite a strong global economy and near full employment, none of the four societal institutions that the study measures – government, business, NGOs and media – is trusted. The cause of this paradox can be found in people's fears about the future and their role in it, which are a wake-up call for our institutions to embrace a new way of effectively building trust: balancing competence with ethical behaviour."

This wake-up call is also a wake-up call for leaders in industry to know that, if you don't already, your role in society is fundamental to rebuilding trust by balancing competence with ethical behaviour in your organisation and how it interacts with society. If you look at my model of collective trust, related to the words 'competence' and 'ethical behaviour' in the Edelman quote, I see 'competence' in 'standard' because both competency and capacity are a part of my meaning of standard. Clearly my model incorporates 'ethical behaviour' in the 'behaviour' quadrant. In a survey done in June 2020, the Edelman Trust Barometer shares that 60% of people responded yes to this statement: "How a brand responds over the next several weeks to the protests against racial injustice will influence whether I buy or boycott them in the future." It is you, the leader in society, that will directly influence this.

I include these quotes from Edelman to give validation to my argument that things are changing in society. As a leader in industry how you observe these changes, have strategies in place – by having made choices on possibilities – and then taking action is so important to how people will trust you personally, as well as how they trust your organisation – both those internally and externally to the organisation.

The relationship between society and trust is changing.

Look at these relative to purpose/intent/standards and behaviours in my framework of collective trust within my overall model and New Ordering of Trust:

- **Purpose** – there seems not to be the common purpose of internationalism that was created at the end of WW2 and has lasted uninterrupted globally until the last five years. Arguably since the end of WW2, and with the nuclear deterrent, this has been the most globally peaceful time in human history – notwithstanding the localised bellicose nature of some countries in all parts of the globe throughout that period.

- **Intent** – the intent in society seems to be moving more to 'about me' than 'about you'. Look at the nationalism that is more predominant in society today than 'yesterday'. I do wonder if post Covid-19, this might shift 'back', given the humanism that has been shown in most parts of the world during the pandemic?

- **Standards** – standards of what is acceptable are changing – in many ways for the good (#MeToo, #BlackLivesMatter) and others not (courtesy, respect for others).

- **Behaviour** – what is an acceptable behaviour is changing in relation to above; some good, some not.

I do acknowledge that culturally there will be different lenses put over these four quadrants in cultures other than the *WEIRD* cultures (western, educated, industrialised, rich, democratic) that I have lived and worked in most of my life. However, I do believe these quadrants are applicable to those that are not WEIRD too, just with different distinctions within them. (WEIRD was first used by Henrich, Heine, & Norenzayan in their paper 'Behavioural and Brain Sciences' 2010).

This collective trust in the society we live in affects the inner circle in the model of how we trust ourselves, as it challenges our stories and narratives that we have grown up with and lived our adult lives with.

Collective trust and the changing world of leadership

The most recent Edelman's 2022 Trust Barometer headline is "Societal leadership is now a core function of business". This year's survey shares that, "at 61%, business is the most trusted institution".

This shift in institutional trust is one of the two key elements of how leadership is changing in my view – as you now know, as a leader you must be more of a leader in society, as well as your team and your business than was ever required before, as trust in the classic institutions of state, media, and church decline. What is new to this edition of the book is the insight that more socially conscious employees now expect you, as their leader, to take a lead on social issues, both publicly and in your organisation. As the Disney Company found out earlier this year when staying quiet on the new legislation in the US that "restricts classroom instruction on sexual orientation and gender identity", when employees walked out on the job based on the company not taking a stance.

However, if you provide an opinion with a societal theme that can also be very risky if not well thought out, aligned with corporate policy and in keeping with the public mood, as Stuart Kirk of HSBC found out recently when accusing "central bankers and policymakers of overstating the financial risks of climate change in an attempt to out-hyperbole the next guy". The result of this statement was a public rebuke from the head of HSBC's wealth and personal banking business, Nuno Matos, as he shared, as reported by the *Australian Financial Review*, that Kirk's views "are inconsistent with HSBC's strategy and do not reflect the views of the senior leadership of HSBC or HSBC Asset Management".

The second way that leadership is changing, in my view, is you having to lead more from the heart than has been required before – not only from the head.

There are more empowered women in general, and more women in 'C Suite' roles (however still not enough) driving a different style; the millennial generation looking for a different style of leadership to the traditional ego-fuelled 'my way or the highway' and 'I have to know it all' approach, and minority groups in business are rightly demanding more inclusion of their views and concerns. Not only for the 'fact' that leadership is changing, but it also needs a different approach because in today's data-driven and more complex business landscape the leaders' role is being expanded into areas not previously demanded of them.

As a CEO you have to adapt to your role being expanded in scope with more ambiguity in business today, as well as take your team/business on a journey of trust, as opposed to you believing you will be trusted as the leader because of your position in the company. This, combined with more working from home and the traditional hierarchical structure in organisations changing to a more agile nature, you and your executives must be more self-aware and use skills that emphasise effective listening, empathy, curiosity, awareness of emotions (both of self and others), relationship building and co-creation of outcomes to augment the more traditional leadership skills of visioning and decision-making.

We have covered all of these attributes of styles of leadership in this book, including through 'types of conversations' in chapter five where you must be able to ask not only, "what you do you think?", but "how are you feeling?", and have the competency in the domain of moods/emotional awareness and literacy (not intelligence) to deal with the response to that question.

As Nicholas Janni shares about the changing nature of leadership: "To survive and thrive they must include yet transcend mindsets and capacities that, while once very effective, now contribute to the problem."

I acknowledge that this is not a leadership book per se, however I want to acknowledge that as a reader of this book, that your world is changing and as such styles of leadership, and leadership choices, need to adapt to meet these changes. By going deeper into the world of trust using my model, distinctions and insights shared, I hope this supports you to acknowledge these changes, and as appropriate, make shifts in both your Way of Being and Doing, to be a more effective leader of self, of your team/ organisation and in society.

Practical application

When thinking about your role as a leader and your role in society, what is your impact on the lives of those who you lead and how do you take that into account when you make your decisions? How does your product or service affect society? How do you trust the society in which you live and lead and how does that influence both your Way of Being and your Way of Doing as a leader? All of this will causally relate to how you are trusted as a leader by the society in which you lead, as well as to your purpose.

The barriers you may face are your unconscious or unknown biases. To help with this you might want to 'take the elevator from your mind to your body' and see what lies within. (See chapter four.)

Collective trust and 'universal energy'

Let's change pace and take this even wider – when I'm able to meditate and feel the 'universal energy', I feel a shared sense of the vast space that I inhabit with every other living being in the world. The paradox of this shared experience when on my own 'with the world' enables me to trust that I'm not alone and that we are all in this together. By having this feeling, it provides the ultimate context for me trusting myself. For you, this might be praying or going to your place of worship – a church, a mosque, a synagogue, a temple, a monastery or even a geographical place such as a river (for example, the Ganges for Hindus). It might be simply meditating and having an existential experience where you are at one with something else. John J Prendergast, a leader in somatic healing and psychotherapy and author of *In Touch*, shared with me and others in a Coaches Rising Transformative Presence coaching workshop in 2019 the idea of "taking the pilgrimage of attention to the soul." This is what I feel is getting in touch with the 'universal energy'.

Alan Watts, known for popularising eastern philosophy in the western world between the 1940s and 1960s, can be heard at the end of a YouTube recording called "Is there a purpose to living" saying this – "here's the choice, are you going to trust it or not? If you do trust it, you may get let down, and this "it" is yourself, your own nature, and all nature around you. There are going to be mistakes, but if you don't trust it all, you're going to strangle yourself. To live, I must have faith. I must trust myself to the totally unknown. I must trust myself to a nature, which does not have a boss".

Rob Bell in his book *Everything is Spiritual* writes:

"There's a line,
And you're over here watching,
And the thing you're watching is over there doing whatever it's going to do,
On the other side of the line.
But we know that there is no line.
There is no out there *out there*.
To witness it is to affect it.
There's only this one reality, and in it everything is connected to everything else."

I reckon these two writers and orators explain my notion of universal energy way better than I can.

For my purposes, and also because I'm in no way qualified or competent to take this any deeper, I ask you to see it as a 'universal energy' that is greater than anything you can personally create or find in yourself, your team or the society that you feel part of. It is there and, if you can trust it (however you want to label "it"), that will give you the ultimate context to collective trust being bigger than you, one other and the team/society elements of collective trust. You are a part of creating this universal energy, it belongs to all of us and we are all a part of it.

In chapter four, I mentioned Jim Dethmer's four states of consciousness and the fourth state, "as me". He shares, in a 2020 Somatic Coaches Rising workshop, that this state "is where the ego has a direct experience of being unified with everything else". This state of being and being in touch with 'universal energy' is my interpretation of Dethmer's "as me".

I accept that, in this domain of 'universal energy', it is more difficult to relate directly to the four quadrants of trust. However, I believe there are elements of common purpose in how you determine universal energy and a common intent to find a higher plane in this space for many. There are common standards for what you choose to believe in, and there is a common behaviour in finding a way to presence yourself and attain this "as me" state of consciousness.

You may not believe in any religion, philosophy or even the science of quantum physics or space. However, you may allow yourself to question what lies beyond earth and your stories. What is that energy, and does that have any relevance to who you are and what you trust?

Practical application

If you want to have a crack at getting in touch with this universal energy that I refer to, use my 'taking the elevator from your mind to your body' practice that I talked about in chapter four. In addition to that, when you focus on your breathing in this exercise, imagine that you are breathing into a balloon. That balloon is the 'universal energy' that every living creature is breathing into, at the same time. As it expands, it may give you trust in this shared feeling that you are not alone and there is something bigger to place your trust in.

Here's another exercise that might help, which I learned from Steven D'Souza, Associate Fellow at Saïd Business School, Oxford University in England, and author of *Brilliant Networking*. I call this the 'I am' exercise. Allow yourself to meditate and 'take the elevator from your mind to your body' by following your breathing. Keep following your breathing and start saying "I am (your name)" say 20 times. (I would say "I am Conor"). You don't have to count the exact number. Keep following your breathing and then say, "I am" 20 times (dropping your name). Then say, "I" 20 times (dropping the word 'am'). After this, drop the 'I' and be at silence with your breathing. See what occurs when you do this. For me, this is a great way of allowing my insignificance as a person, when related to 'universal energy', to shine through and to open myself up to possibilities. It is not about me or my ego. It is simply about being present and in a space of becoming. Thomas Hubl, a spiritual teacher, leading trauma coach, founder of the Academy of Inner Science and author of *Healing Collective Trauma*, referred to this place of presence as "the birthplace of the future as well as the integration of the past", in the Transformative Coaching Programme, through Coaches Rising in 2019.

Spend time in this space, that is the 'now'. In it, there is nothing to prove, nobody to beat, no one doing anything 'to' you, no problem to solve. It simply 'is'.

The only real barrier here is allowing yourself to go this deep in your thinking and/or your meditating. It is a choice and it does take practise. Perhaps you could listen to an app to help you in this space, such as Calm, Smiling Mind or Headspace or Waking Up. You might want to try yoga to support yourself in finding this space of 'universal energy'.

If you want to go deeper into this space, you can see that my personal learning has come from the wisdom of Sieler, Watts, Hubl, Prendergast, Dethmer, D'Souza, Blake, Whyte, Bell, and no doubt others who I have yet to discover!

Trust in self – the outer circle

Ultimately trust begins and ends with self. If my book ended with talking about 'universal energy', it wouldn't fully portray my thesis that trust begins and ends with self.

CO'M model and Ordering of Trust

I'm going to be bold enough now, at the end of this book, to use my model and New Ordering of trust, along with the models, writings, references to others and stories that I've shared with you as my evidence of this.

You begin by understanding your **stories** and making meaning of them, looking for the **assessments** you are making in amongst the **assertions** of your life's journey. Your stories are an input to you becoming the observer of **your Way of Being** and trusting it, which is in the domains of **your language in your head, your moods, and your physiology.** You then move to trusting **your Way of Doing**, which includes your audible language, your behaviour and **consistently delivering on your commitments.** The outcome is your **brand and reputation** when related to trust.

You feel **in flow** when you trust both your Way of Being and your Way of Doing. You trust others by risking something you value, being appropriately vulnerable and choosing to be vulnerable to their actions, as well as holding them as **'the legitimate other'**, gaining a commitment from them, holding them accountable to your standards and timelines by using appropriate **'types of conversations'**, and asking them to feed that progress to you. You **build relationships** by making it about them, not about you (i.e. being invested in their concerns sincerely). You **consistently deliver on your commitments to yourself and others.** You find and create a **Collective Trust** using **purpose, intent, standards and behaviours** in the realm of **team, society, and universal energy.**

If you do all that, it comes right back at you. This is the deeper meaning of trust that I shared on the opening page of chapter one.

Do you trust yourself to do all this work in the space of trust? If you do, then you've got it. My model and a New Ordering of Trust which shows that **trust begins and ends with self.**

Global coaching initiative update

I shared with you earlier in the chapter that I would update you 'in real time' about the Global Coaching Initiative. I do this because "trust begins and ends with self", and if I didn't share this, as the book was about to be published, I wouldn't be personally living and demonstrating everything that I have written for you in this book. So, I have pulled back the book from the publisher to write this.

On 5 November 2020, I decided to step back from leading the Global Coaching Initiative because, at a headline level, 'coaches want to coach', and that is what I set out to do nearly four years ago when leaving executive leadership. I found that I was leading this initiative, for the last six months, with all of my Way of Being and Doing, with an incredible group of amazing and talented people, but it was draining me and drawing me from my soul and heart of what I set out to do – which is to coach, not lead. More than this, I want to show you how I came to my decision and how it relates to trust. Shown below is my whiteboard that was progressively filled in at 0415hrs on that morning in my study. Having been sitting with this very uncomfortable feeling for weeks, I decided I needed to make 'a call', especially as we had a contract to sign that would really have moved us from the planning phase to the implementation phase. I was asking myself, on behalf of this partner firm which we were about to sign a contract with, could I deliver to a RISCC assessment of me being trustworthy or pass the test of 'does this person (me) deliver on his commitment to my expectations – stated or not – with the intent of supporting me and taking care of my concerns?'. I wasn't sure that I could. (The RISCC above refers to the five assessments of trust that I used in the first edition of the book which excluded 'vulnerable' and 'consistent').

The only way I could really know, feel and sense if stepping back was the 'right' thing for me (and the organisation) to do, was to self-coach myself and seek counsel from others. The whiteboard is me sharing with you, in about the most vulnerable way a person can, my own process that morning. Without going into it all, I hope having read this book that you can see on display my New Ordering of Trust 'put through its paces' for and by myself. The counsel, and coaching from others, around this time helped greatly; however, it was this hour and a half, using the distinctions shared in this book, that brought me to my conclusion.

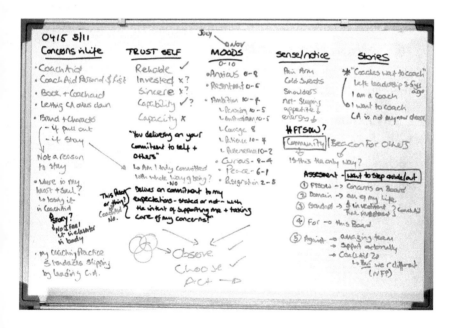

The outcome was, following that self-coaching session on 5 November 2020, I shared with the Directors of the initiative that I was stepping aside. The response I received from each of them was humbling and something I will never forget. After a collective

Directors' meeting, I then shared my decision with the rest of the organisation, over the next two days, and got the same response.

The following week I shared my decision with those external to the organisation and got the same humbling responses.

The team is now reconsidering their options and I wish them well in serving others, as we set out to do, if that is their choice.

Conclusion

You've learned about collective trust, its four components and how it relates to my model and New Ordering of Trust. You've learned that collective trust is in the domains of team, society, and 'universal energy'. At the end, I brought it all back to trust in self by recapping my model and New Ordering of Trust, both theoretically and practically, in a very personal way.

Can you now step outside how you trust yourself and another by looking at trust in a collective way – your trust in team, your society and universal energy? Reflect on these outer circles and allow yourself to see trust differently and how it then all comes back to you.

Trust begins and ends with self.

CO'M model and Ordering of Trust

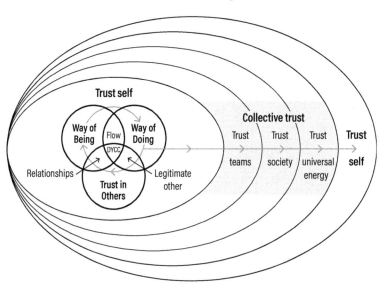

Conclusion

You have learned that trust begins and ends with self.

You have learned my meaning of Trust:

"That you consistently deliver on your commitments, both to self and others."

You have learned that trust is an assessment in the domains of 'being' and doing'.

You have learned about the Seven Assessments of Trust. You have learned the distinction between Way of Being and Way of Doing.

You have learned how to use the model, and the seven assessments of trust, to mitigate risk in your life regarding trust.

You have learned how to find flow in your life, how to legitimise others and how to build more effective relationships.

You have learned about collective trust and the importance of your role in society as a leader.

You have learned how leadership is changing and the role trust plays in that change.

You have learned how to apply collective trust in a very practical way, from my '0415hrs session'.

By putting into practice the learnings in this book, your life and role as a leader will be more fulfilling.

As a leader, you will coordinate action more effectively through language with less time and lower cost to get things done. You will observe yourself in the moment more and shift your mood or your physiology to listen better, be more open to possibilities, more curious and more trusted by those who choose to follow you.

When you truly trust yourself, you have more fulfilling relationships. Life will be easier as you will be more in flow, and you will have more techniques to draw on when you find yourself 'below the line', which we all do.

Now what?

My thanks to Rob and Kristen Bell for bringing this question "now what?" to me from their *RobCast* of 19 October 2020. It feels the right question to ask now, to finish the book.

At the helicopter level, draw from my coaching and life framework of Observe|Choose|Act and relate it to trust:

- **Observe** – Observe your Way of Being in your inner (self) language, moods, and physiology. Observe your Way of Doing in relation to the actions you take (including the audible language that you use), your behaviours and how those actions impact your brand and how you legitimise others as well as the strength of your relationships. Ask yourself #FTSOW in the moment to give you self-accountability and to help answer what type of conversation you're going to have and what you want from it. Ask yourself, "Are my requests and offers open to the scrutiny of the commitment cycle?" Observe your role as a team leader in society using the collective trust model. Observe the environment you are leading in, knowing this observation comes from within you, however it is still critical. Observe yourself and your relationship to universal energy.

- **Choose** – Are you open to possibilities and choices by being 'above the line' and being okay with uncertainty and, at times, not knowing?
- **Act** – Take action from a place of flow or 'through me'. Ask yourself, "Do I consistently deliver on my commitments to myself and others, every time, using the Seven Assessments of Trust?"

If you do all that every day, you will trust yourself and others will trust you. You will find the meaning of "trust begins and ends with self".

When you fail, which you sometimes will, forgive yourself, learn from it and go again.

Can I do that?

Yes you can, if you choose to. The obstacles to Observe|Choose| Act, and knowing that trust begins and ends with self, are all in the self. Consider the opening stanza from David Whyte's poem, *Start Close In*:[1]

> *Start close in,*
> *don't take the second step*
> *or the third,*
> *start with the first*
> *thing*
> *close in,*
> *the step*
> *you don't want to take.*

---

[1] Printed with permission from Many Rivers Press, davidwhyte.com. *Start Close In* by David Whyte, from *River Flow and David Whyte: Essentials* © Many Rivers Press, Langley, WA USA.

My meaning of this is – start close in, take the step you don't want to take, just take the first step and trust what follows.

This poem moved me when I heard it orated live by David in 2019, and it took me, at that time, to what I knew I had already done – started close in, taken the first step, the one I didn't want to take, and trusted in my choices thereafter. Once you choose to do this, obstacles will lessen, things will serendipitously unfold for you and you will find that trust begins and ends with self. That will lead to a more fulfilling life, both professionally and personally.

By reading this book, I hope that you as a leader in society, and more generally that the leaders of today, are more trusting of self and more trusted by others. I hope that you, and they, are more focused on others and not self, more focused on legacy than ego, are more aware of your, and their, critical role in society and, most importantly, that you (and they) lead a more fulfilled life by using my model and New Ordering of Trust every day.

My purpose in life is 'to be a beacon for others' and if I can be that beacon for you, by being your caddy as I walk alongside you, it would be my privilege.

Index

References

Introduction

https://www.alanwatts.org/

Chapter One

https://parksaustralia.gov.au/uluru/discover/culture/stories/mala-story/
Rachel Botsman, *Who Can You Trust?* (2017)
Charles Feltman, *The Thin Book of Trust* (2008)
Ashkan Tashvir, *Human Being* (2022) page 92.
https://www.dictionary.com/browse/trust
https://www.britannica.com/topic/ontology-metaphysics
Alan Sieler – *Coaching to the Human Soul volume one* (2003) page 241.
https://trustedadvisor.com/why-trust-matters/understanding-trust/
    understanding-the-trust-equation
https://haradevelopment.org/
https://hbr.org/2006/09/the-decision-to-trust
https://www.speedoftrust.com/#videos
https://medium.com/@ameet/the-four-cores-of-trust-52248c27eb16
https://www.forbes.com/sites/prudygourguechon/2018/02/20/
    why-inspiring-trust-and-trusting-others-are-essential-leadership-
    capacities-within-bounds/#7f55de415359
Gabrielle Dolan – *Real Communication* (2019) page 6.
https://www.disney.com.au/movies/the-lion-king
https://www.nationalgeographic.com/magazine/2015/07/gandhi-
    legacy-india/

Chapter Two

Bill Ash – *Redesigning Conversations* (2022) page 51.
Alan Sieler – *Coaching to the Human Soul volume one* (2003) page 293.
Robert Kegan, *In Over Our Heads: The mental demands of modern life* (1998).
http://conversationsforaction.com/
https://actionable.co/blog/2016/11/careful-distinguish-fact-opinion/
https://www.victoriawalks.org.au/Assets/Files/5641%20VWI%20Smart%20Steps%20Lesson%20Plan%20English%20L5%20FINAL.pdf
Alan Sieler – *Coaching to the Human Soul volume one* (2003) pages 351–355.
https://www.ted.com/speakers/carol_dweck
Bill Ash – *Redesigning Conversations* (2022) page 53.
https://www.forbes.com/sites/sunniegiles/2018/05/09/how-vuca-is-reshaping-the-business-environment-and-what-it-means-for-innovation/#59df224feb8d
https://fs.blog/2015/03/carol-dweck-mindset/
https://hbr.org/2016/01/what-having-a-growth-mindset-actually-means
https://thetrustambassador.com/2015/11/21/delegation-and-trust/
https://hbr.org/2007/11/a-leaders-framework-for-decision-making
https://www.awm.gov.au/sites/default/files/Audacity.pdf
https://www.gordontraining.com/free-workplace-articles/learning-a-new-skill-is-easier-said-than-done/

Chapter Three

https://hbr.org/2020/05/begin-with-trust
Alan Sieler – *Coaching to the Human Soul volume one* (2003) page 8.
Amanda Blake – *Whole Body-Mind Coaching in Coaches Rising: Neuroscience of Change* (2019). Truckee, CA: Embright, LLC.
https://www.washingtonpost.com/politics/2020/01/17/trump-has-broken-more-promises-than-hes-kept/

Chapter Four

Alan Sieler – *Coaching to the Human Soul volume two* (2007) page 148.
Alan Sieler – *Coaching to the Human Soul volume one* (2003) page 31.

Ashkan Tashvir, *Human Being* (2022) pages 88, 275 and 276.

http://conversationsforaction.com/history/language-action-theory

Alan Sieler – *Coaching to the Human Soul volume one* (2003) page 140.

https://www.justgiving.com/fundraising/simonomalley

Robert C. Solomon, *The Passions* (1976, republished 1993), page 23.

Robert C. Solomon, *The Passions* (1976, republished 1993), page 71.

Dan Newby and Curtis Watkins – *The Field Guide to Emotions* (2019) page 6.

https://schoolofemotions.world/

Susan David with Brené Brown https://brenebrown.com/podcast/brene-with-dr-susan-david-on-the-dangers-of-toxic-positivity-part-1-of-2/.

Alan Sieler – *Coaching to the Human Soul volume two* (2007) page 148.

Robert C. Solomon, *The Passions* (1976, republished 1993), page 60.

https://www.linkedin.com/posts/conoromalley_observechooseact-becurious-forthesakeofwhat-activity-6717590708569669632-IVoP

https://conscious.is/about

Alan Sieler – *Coaching to the Human Soul volume two* (2007) page 193.

Amanda Blake, *Your Body is Your Brain* (2019)

https://www.coachesrising.com/

Nicholas Janni, *Leader as Healer* (2022).

http://www.online-literature.com/james_joyce/964/

https://www.researchgate.net/publication/254412101_Exploring_intuition_and_its_role_in_managerial_decision_making/link/5463757a0cf2837efdb30bef/download

https://qbi.uq.edu.au/brain/brain-anatomy/what-neuron

https://www.ninds.nih.gov/Disorders/Patient-Caregiver-Education/Life-and-Death-Neuron

https://monoskop.org/images/3/35/Maturana_Humberto_Varela_Francisco_Autopoiesis_and_Congition_The_Realization_of_the_Living.pdf

https://www.britannica.com/topic/cogito-ergo-sum

https://hbr.org/2017/01/the-neuroscience-of-trust

https://hbr.org/2016/11/a-simple-way-to-stay-grounded-in-stressful-moments

https://drchatterjee.com/book/
https://quoteinvestigator.com/2010/07/14/luck/

Chapter Five

https://www.youtube.com/watch?v=u4ZoJKF_VuA
Alan Sieler – *Coaching to the Human Soul volume one* (2003) page 265.
https://www.dictionary.com/browse/request?s=ts
https://www.ccl.org/
Genevieve Hawkins – *Mentally at Work* (2020) page 135.
Alan Sieler – *Coaching to the Human Soul volume one* (2003) page 255.
Ila Edgar – *Trust on Purpose* Podcast. Episode – "Strengthen trust with Clear and Complete Requests", 8th August 2022.
Brian Hartzer, *The Leadership Star* (2021), page 75.
http://www.espn.com/sportscentury/athletes.html
http://www.apbr.org/oldtimrs.html
https://www.businessinsider.com.au/how-nikes-air-jordan-brand-got-name-jordans-agent-2020-4
https://twitter.com/StephenRCovey/status/1132647935391535104?s=19
https://www.stevenkotler.com/rabbit-hole/frequently-asked-questions-on-flow
https://positivepsychology.com/mihaly-csikszentmihalyi-father-of-flow/
https://www.bbc.com/sport/formula1/53800895
https://www.jessicaennis.net/contact-1 – contact made to verify quote
https://conscious.is/about

Chapter Six

https://leadingwithtrust.com/2012/01/29/three-circles-of-trust/
https://www.linkedin.com/posts/conoromalley_becurious-observe chooseact-ceocaddy-activity-6922357331540291584-bmva?utm_source=linkedin_share&utm_medium=member_desktop_web
Alan Sieler – *Coaching to the Human Soul volume one* (2003) page 123.
Alan Sieler – *Coaching to the Human Soul volume one* (2003) page 124.
https://www.talkingabout.com.au/4TheLegitimateOther
https://brenebrown.com/podcast/brene-with-charles-feltman-on-trust-building-maintaining-and-restoring-it/

https://www.linkedin.com/posts/chyonne_listening-for-leaders-activity-6704517210527952896-gdZP
https://wholebodylistening.org/about/
https://www.linkedin.com/posts/conoromalley_observechooseact-becurious-mentoring-activity-6715072293170765825-_MVM
Martin G. Moore – *No Bullsh!t Leadership* (2021), page 152.
https://hbr.org/2019/07/to-be-happier-at-work-invest-more-in-your-relationships
Genevieve Hawkins – *Mentally at Work* (2020) page 15.
https://hbr.org/2017/10/to-be-a-great-leader-you-have-to-learn-how-to-delegate-well
http://www3.weforum.org/docs/WEF_FOJ_Executive_Summary_Jobs.pdf
William Cowan, *Building a Winning Career* (2021)
Blenheim Partners, No Limitations Podcast – episode 97 Tim Ford, Make Every Day Count.

Chapter Seven

https://www.hbs.edu/faculty/Pages/item.aspx?num=59637
https://hbr.org/2017/08/high-performing-teams-need-psychological-safety-heres-how-to-create-it
https://www.ausfoodnews.com.au/2008/08/25/national-foods-wins-race-for-dairy-farmers-with-910-million-bid.html
https://www.prnewswire.co.uk/news-releases/bt-and-poet-laureate-simon-armitage-unveil-something-clicked-a-reflection-of-life-in-2020-to-mark-national-poetry-day-873191336.html
https://www.cisl.cam.ac.uk/resources/sustainability-leadership/about/leadership-hub
https://coachaid20.com/
https://www.edelman.com/trustbarometer
https://www2.psych.ubc.ca/~henrich/pdfs/WeirdPeople.pdf
https://www.nytimes.com/2022/03/22/business/media/disney-florida-employee-protests.html
https://www.edelman.com/sites/g/files/aatuss191/files/2022-01/Trust%2022_Top10.pdf

https://www.afr.com/companies/financial-services/hsbc-suspends-
   banker-over-climate-change-comments-20220523-p5anme?utm_
   content=AROUND_THE_WORLD&list_name=EBE726C6-38DF-
   4725-9BE4-5091999D8384&promote_channel=edmail&utm_
   campaign=the-brief&utm_medium=email&utm_source=
   newsletter&utm_term=2022-05-23&mbnr=MjMxMDQ0MTQ&in
   stance=2022-05-23-12-33-AEST&jobid=29389668
https://www.nicholasjanni.com/core-presence/
https://www.youtube.com/watch?v=21RwqnB8GrE&ab_channel=
   theJourneyofPurposeTJOP
Rob Bell – *Everything Is Spiritual* (2020) page 159.

Now what?

https://robbell.podbean.com/e/now-what-1602624905/
https://www.davidwhyte.com/events/2020/5/3/start-close-in-a-
   weekend-with-david-whyte

Books referred to, but not referenced by page

Martin Heidegger *Being and Time* (1927)
Fernando Flores *Understanding Computers and Cognition* (1986)
Stephen M.R. Covey *The SPEED of Trust* (2006) and *Smart Trust* (2011)
Stephen R. Covey *The 7 Habits of Highly Effective People* (1989)
Hector Garcia and Francesc Miralles Ikigai *The Japanese Secret to a
   Long and Happy Life* (2016)
Jean-Paul Sartre *La Nausee* (1938)
Humberto Maturana and Franciso Varela *Autopoiesis and Cognition:
   The Realization of the Living* (1972)
Dr. Dan Siegel *The Developing Mind* (1999)
Amanda Blake *Your Body is Your Brain* (2019)
Mihaly Csikszentmihalyi *Flow: The Psychology of Optimal Experience*
   (1990)
Steven D'Souza *Brilliant Networking* (2007)
John J Prendergast *In Touch* (2015)
Thomas Hubl *Healing Collective Trauma* (November 2020)

conoromalley.com.au